OB
Diary

STEVEN PHILLIPS

CONTENTS

PREFACE i

1 VOLTAIRE STREET 1

2 THE ORGY KING 16

3 BASSLIPS MCLAREN 26

4 TALES FROM THE BAT CAVE 36

5 PESCADERO TRAGEDY 48

6 MA KELLOGG 57

7 BIG WEDNESDAY 68

8 DECKHANDS 80

9 MEXICO 94

10 CHURCH ROW 105

11 THE LAST LUAU 116

12 LOBSTERMAN 125

13 HARD TIMES 138

14 THE WORLD CLOSES IN 146

EPILOGUE 156

PREFACE

I was fortunate to grow up in Ocean Beach during what I consider the Golden Years. OB was a self-contained village of young families of modest means. You didn't need a car; everything a family needed could be had in the central business district anchored by Newport Avenue. It was a typical small town where everybody knew each other. On hot summer nights we slept with the doors and windows open; our security consisted of a latched screen door. The beach that stretched from the foot of Newport Avenue to the Mission Bay entrance channel was enjoyed only by locals and an occasional group of sailors from the Naval Training Center just over the hill. During the winter months the beach was mostly deserted.

The tidepools south of Newport Avenue were rich with sea life: Abalone, starfish, crabs, sea anemones and small fish populated the clear pool waters during low tides. Game fish were abundant offshore and in the still waters of bays and estuaries. Surfing was in its infancy in those days. Local pioneers riding surfboards made of wood explored the reefs of Sunset Cliffs, bestowing colorful names on the best breaks. The crew of pioneers was small and tight knit. Crowded waves were not a problem then; finding someone to surf with often was.

Ocean Beach has always been home to some very colorful characters, even in the Golden Years. Many of my friends growing up came direct from Central Casting; real life heroes and villains, odd balls, drunks, and comedians. Surrounded by the sea, it is no wonder that surfing, fishing, diving and boating would play a dominant role in our lives. All of us have tales to tell from those years; from that perfect day of six-foot glassy waves, to some hair-raising brushes with death at the other extreme.

The Texas Longhorn, oddly enough, was the identifying symbol of the Golden Years in OB; at least for the young and rowdy. Images of Longhorns were everywhere; scrawled on car doors, fences, stuck to bumpers, and neatly drawn and lettered on the windows of certain Newport Avenue businesses. OB locals caught up in the Vietnam draft left Longhorn symbols carved or scrawled everywhere they went. It was an informal brotherhood consisting of territorial surfers, ordinary resident natives, and a handful of thugs that were uniquely rooted in, and protective of, the Ocean Beach homeland.

OB DIARY

1 VOLTAIRE STREET

The House on Voltaire

My family migrated to California from rural Indiana in 1952. We made the eventful trip west on Route 66 with two other young families. A mysterious encounter at road's end in Santa Monica resulted in us scrapping our planned destination of San Francisco and heading south to San Diego instead. There, we found a beach town that would be our new forever home. The little village of Ocean Beach had everything the family needed, all within walking distance. The neighborhood was full of young families with kids my age, and I quickly made several new friends. Like me, most of them had recently arrived from elsewhere, usually from somewhere in the

Midwest. We settled first in an ocean front duplex in a government housing project known as Azure Vista. The project was slated for demolition, so in a year or so we moved a mile north into Ocean Beach.

Our new home on Voltaire Street was built from a kit sold by Sears Roebuck and sat on a lot in a commercial zone. It was a two-bedroom craftsman, three blocks from the beach and two blocks from the San Diego River. There were two bars on our block. The Boots 'n Saddle was a swinging dive bar directly across the street. Most nights I fell asleep to the sound of honky-tonk music and breaking glass. The Brown Bottle was just down the street and was frequented by an older, quieter, crowd. In the middle of the block was a liquor store, Liticker's Liquor. Right next door to our house was the Bayview Nursery, and next to the nursery was Plummer's Minerals; a store for the hard core rockhounds that scoured the backcountry in those days looking for uranium.

My parents' rocky marriage came to an end shortly after the birth of my twin brothers. Dad left San Diego and disappeared somewhere in the south with his new girlfriend. It would be several years before we heard from him again. I had to step in and help mom with my younger siblings; I was 12 years old. To help make ends meet, I delivered the morning paper seven days a week. I delivered the main drag of Newport Avenue, and the neighborhood to the north that paralleled the beach. My route was a jumble of small homes, apartments, and courts. I finished my route at daybreak on Newport. By that time, the numerous Newport dive bars would open their doors and begin cleaning for the day ahead. The stench of stale beer and cigarette smoke hung in the air outside bars with names like Pacific Shores, Bamboo Inn, and Tony's.

The last paper of the day was delivered in person to "Pete" Peterson at the Ocean Beach Bake Shop. I'd tap on the window, and Pete would come out of the kitchen to let me in. Pete started baking for the day in the wee hours of the morning, so by the time I showed up the cooling racks were full. I went in the back and selected two Danish from the cooling rack, then sat on a stool at the lunch counter where Pete had a 12-ounce Coke waiting for me.

Lawrence "Pete" Peterson

Most mornings I was joined by several other neighborhood paperboys who delivered the OB routes next to mine. We all loved Pete; he was always kind to our unruly daybreak entourage, and his pastry creations were out of this world. My mother walked to Newport Avenue to shop twice a week. She bought freshly baked bread from the Bake Shop in whole loaves. Bread for sandwiches was placed in a bread slicing machine and bagged for the trip home. Occasionally, she returned with whole loaves to immediately re heat, slice thick, and slather with butter and jam.

I struck up friendships with several of the morning Bake Shop crew. Among them was John Finlay, a kid who had one of the neighboring routes. John lived just two blocks up from me on Voltaire with his mom and sister. It seemed like most of the kids in Ocean Beach were being raised by a single parent. Navy households usually had two parents, but dad was deployed most of the time to the Western Pacific. We were all renters and more times than not our landlords lived in the large ocean view homes of upper OB and Point Loma.

The owner of Liticker's Liquor was a kind old man who stocked his unique store according to his personal interests. One aisle in the small store was dedicated to things like chocolate covered bugs, smoked octopus, sturgeon roe, and other odd stuff found nowhere else in Ocean Beach. Mister Liticker stocked fishing gear; rods, reels, and assorted tackle. Mounted on the wall above the cash register was a marlin head mount, his first and only Marlin. He knew I didn't have a father at home and was always attentive when I came into the store. He became like a surrogate grandpa to me. We soon developed a friendship that revolved around our mutual love of fishing. Every Christmas I got to pick out a new rod and reel. For my birthday there was always something new for my tackle box. I always stopped by the store on my way home from fishing to show off my catch. He was a rare adult I felt at ease talking to. He often asked how things were going at home. He never talked down to me. He sat in his chair at eye level and spoke to me like I was an adult.

My dad didn't drink much, but when he did it was always a weekend binge. Toward the end it was not unusual for him to leave Friday evening for a pack of cigarettes and return Sunday afternoon. My Mom, a staunch Baptist, considered him an alcoholic and blamed most of their marital problems on alcohol. I was raised to detest alcohol and be wary of anyone who imbibed. I openly expressed these sentiments to Mister Liticker. I remember his advice to me:

"I don't want to scare you Stevie, but life gets a lot harder as you grow older. Mixed in with all the wonderful things you will experience will be great sadness and hard times; that's true for everyone, including people who seem to be happy all the time. Just love everyone and don't judge; most folks are doing the best they can fighting battles you can't see."

I always made sure I had two leftover newspapers, one of which I gave to Mister Liticker, and the other to a younger store owner named Chris who had just opened a business two blocks from my home. Chris had brought a concept to Ocean Beach that was unique in that day; a combination liquor store and Delicatessen. We had never seen monster sandwiches like this before. I became an instant fan of Deli fare and bartered the daily newspaper for an occasional Hot Pastrami or Reuben. Chris was breaking new ground. In the years that followed, liquor store delis began popping up all over San Diego. The site he chose for his new business was the most heavily traveled intersection in Ocean Beach; the first thing you see entering or leaving the community. It was a huge success from the get-go.

Chris hired an old coot named Lou to be his right-hand man. Lou wore coveralls and had a contraption he kept in the cooler room. All the kids who came into the store were told it held a caged, vicious Mongoose Of course, we all took the bait and begged to see it. We were led to a dark corner of the walk-in cooler where a heavy wooden crate sat atop a stepstool. The lid had a chicken wire window through which you could safely view the snarling beast. We were invited to lean over the crate and see for ourselves. At the right moment, Lou yanked a cord hidden behind the shelving and screamed at the top of his lungs. The cord released a huge spring holding the lid closed and launched a dirty stuffed Mongoose into our terrified faces.

After we all wised up, Lou had to come up with something else. Chris' stocked something we had never seen anywhere else; Ginger Beer. Lou told us it was the only beer that could be bought by minors, and if we ever tried it, do it secretly at home where we would be safe. Of course, we took the bait…again. Bobby Byrom was one of my rowdier buddies. Together we hatched a plan to buy a 6 pack each and get crocked in the safety of my bedroom on Voltaire Street. When we came to buy the hooch, Lou was suspiciously delighted. We started drinking around noon. The stuff tasted soapy and awful. After a half-hour, we had consumed all the beer. Bobby was sober and doubled over with abdominal pain. I was on the toilet with sudden onset diarrhea. As soon as we were able, we walked the two blocks to Chris' looking pale and distressed, and pissed. Lou had seen us coming. He was laughing like a hyena and holding his sides; tears rolled down his wrinkled cheeks.

Chris Stavros

Ocean Beach in those days was a fishing paradise. The San Diego River had recently been hemmed in by rock jetties to control flooding, creating a placid lagoon loaded with fish. The river was now known as the flood control channel, or simply *The Flood Control* to locals. There was a bait shop, A-1 Bait & Tackle, a few hundred feet from my favorite fishing hole. When the shop was built, a bridge over to Mission Beach on the other side of the river drew hundreds of anglers. The bridge was gone now, but the bait shop was still hanging on.

The bait shop walls were covered with faded photos of the giant croaker and halibut taken by bridge anglers in earlier days. The A-1 was owned by a family who lived in the rear of the shop. A bell on the door jingled when you entered. Soon, a sheet hung in the doorway to the back room would part and out came the owner. When the doorway sheet parted glimpses of the family's living room revealed an old chair and sofa, and lots of kids watching a small black and white TV with rabbit ears.

The owner was a nice man with a bald head and nasty scar above his ear. He saw me staring and explained that a rock had fallen on his head in a well-digging accident. He was partially paralyzed on one side and didn't have the use of his left arm. The family car was a tank-like Hudson and was often seen around the neighborhood crammed with the entire clan. On Sundays, while dad was tending the store, the kids went to church walking single file with mom in the lead. Mom and the kids all wore matching black Keds high top tennis shoes.

The Flood Control lagoon became my favorite place to be. I usually stopped at A-1 for a quarter's worth of fresh razor clams, then climbed up and over the jetty rocks to my fishing hole. The underwater nooks and crannies created by the pile of granite boulders became a haven for a dazzling variety of fish. Every few days I would catch something I'd never seen before. I looked forward to taking my catch to my friend at A-1 Bait for identification.

There were a couple of fish among them that were capable of inflicting great pain. The Sculpin is a red fish with an enormous head and small body. It's head and body are festooned with poisonous spines. I pulled my first Sculpin out of its lair in the boulders late one afternoon. I was fascinated by its odd body and striking color. When I grabbed the fish to remove the hook it went into a frenzy that left me with five deep puncture wounds in my right hand. By the time I got home my hand was swollen to the size of a boxing glove. The pain was excruciating. Beach doctors knew about Sculpins; Dr. Greaves was there 15 minutes after being called. I sat at the kitchen table with my hand immersed in scalding water and Epsom salts until late that night when the pain was reduced to a throb that persisted for the next three days. I had learned my lesson about handling Sculpin. It wouldn't be long before I found out about stingrays.

Moody's A-1 Bait & Tackle

I shared my adventures at the Flood Control with my morning crew at the OB Bake Shop. I showed them the cave I had found under the granite boulders that made up the jetty. Someone before us had left a deck of cards when they moved on. On the back of each playing card was a different grainy black and white photo of men and women having sex. The men wore hard black shoes with black sox and nothing else. The women all looked like my old Aunt Frieda and appeared to be enduring the experience rather than enjoying it. Along with the cards, we found an old yellowed paperback titled *Hot Pants Miriam*. The story contained no cuss words but spoke of quivering love pudding, throbbing this and that, and so on.

A few hundred feet west of my fishing hole the jetty rocks transitioned to a crescent sand beach that curved into the main channel and ended in a point creating a deep sand bottom pond. It too was loaded with fish. The placid cove was frequented by other anglers from the neighborhood. A group of old men showed up nearly every morning in their beat-up cars to drink alcohol and fish for sand bass. The point at the north end of the crescent lagoon was the honey hole, and the old coots considered it theirs. One old guy appeared to be the leader. His friends called him McLaren. He had a massive belly that his stained tee shirt never completely covered. His jaw was huge and protruded forward of the rest of his face. Large lips jutted out above the jaw, giving him the profile of a trophy seabass.

I came home after a morning of fishing to find mom crying over a letter from home. She had gotten word from her sister in Indiana that Grandpa Cook was gravely ill and that she should come home right away. Mom had earned two weeks of paid vacation by that time. The decision was made to go back to Indiana. We were able to hitch a ride with a couple from Terre Haute in early August. We drove straight through on Route 66 in a packed sedan eating Vienna sausage and saltine crackers and catching catnaps at rest areas. We arrived at the farm in Paris Crossing in time to spend a week with grandpa before he was admitted to a Columbus hospital to be placed in an oxygen tent.

Our second week there was spent in and out of the hospital. I was able to stay with my cousin Dennis for a couple of days and enjoy some catfishing in the creek that ran behind his house near Columbus. There were large catfish that populated a hole at the bend in the creek. We dug up a can of worms and cut several hot dogs into bite size pieces for bait. We sat under a huge sycamore by the slow-moving creek for hours without a nibble; we decided to reel in the lines and go home for dinner. My line was snagged on something. When I pulled hard to break the line something pulled back; it was a fish, a big one. I struggled with the beast for ten minutes before we got a glimpse of it; an enormous catfish that appeared to be around twenty pounds. I just happen to have my Brownie box camera I had brought to take photos of the Indiana kinfolk. I held the squirming giant up and Dennis snapped pictures, then released it back into the creek. It was the highpoint of an otherwise grim vacation.

On the day we left for home I went with mom to the hospital for one last visit. Grandpa was in an oxygen tent, pale and semi-conscious. He acknowledged mom with a finger squeeze when it was time to leave. We arrived back in Ocean Beach on a Saturday. My mother went back to her job at Cubic Corporation on Monday. She was back at noon and in tears; Grandpa Cook had died earlier that morning. Returning for the funeral was out of the question. Mom was distraught and there was nothing I could do to make it better.

It was a full moon night. My bedroom window looked to the east and perfectly framed the cold blue moon. Grandpa was the first death in the family for me. I lay on my pillow staring at the moon, knowing it was the same moon shining over the Dodd Funeral Home in Paris Crossing where Grandpa now lay. I knew every detail of the room. For years the Dodd Funeral Home had the only telephone in town. When a call came in for someone in the family one of the Dodd kids would be sent to fetch us while the caller waited. The phone was in a vestibule outside the viewing room where a former neighbor occasionally lay in repose, surrounded by flowers and loud weeping.

My little sister was four years old and my twin brothers two. They were all on my bed the next morning when I woke up, giggling and tickling each other and me. They were spared the pain of the moment. To them it was just another beautiful Tuesday morning in Ocean Beach. I kept them occupied in the back yard all morning to give Mom space to grieve. I found a letter in the mailbox around noon. It was from my cousin Dennis, and it contained photos of the catfish. I had left the film roll from my Brownie in Columbus to be developed. One of the photos captured the big catfish perfectly. I couldn't wait to show Grandpa Liticker my trophy cat and tell him about Grandpa Cook.

I went down to the store where I was greeted by a family member working the counter. He told me to go to the back office, that Grandma Liticker wanted to talk to me. I sensed something was wrong. I went back and plopped down in a side chair. Mrs. Liticker reached out for my hand and told me in the most loving way possible that Mister Liticker had died. He passed away suddenly the day after we left for Indiana. She opened the top desk drawer and handed me an envelope: Inside the envelope was a hundred-dollar bill and a photo of my first Flood Control fish; a buttermouth perch, with Sam the store cat and mister Liticker.

"Grandpa" Liticker, 1958

2 THE ORGY KING

Late Summer Electrical Storm Over the Jetty

Two weeks after losing Grandpa Cook and Mister Liticker I fell into a deep depression. I went to my happy place on the Flood Control jetty. An early September thunderstorm added to the bleakness of the scene. A fierce wind had whipped the lagoon surface into dingy foam that piled several inches high against the bank.   In the sea of foam floated tumbleweeds and trash herded into the lagoon by the whipping wind. It was an utterly hopeless moment playing out in slow motion. Over the ocean an advancing black wall of clouds lit up by flashes of lightning delineated a fast approaching squall line.

Something sticking up in the flotsam caught my attention; it was a human head.   I scurried down the jetty onto the sand and walked to within earshot of the fool in the water. It was dark, thundering and pouring rain now. The head in the water had watched me approach and was peering at me; only the eyes were visible. I shouted out a warning. As the head emerged from the water, I could see right away he was a young man and certainly wasn't from these parts. His forearms and face were tanned olive, but the rest of his chunky body was alabaster white. He wore only cutoff pants. He had thick black hair and looked a bit like Elvis Presley. I yammered about the peril he was putting himself in by swimming in an electrical storm. He said nothing but kept approaching in silence. I introduced myself as Steve. He passed by in silence heading for the dirt road to town. He stopped and turned around to complete the introduction; "Hello Steve. I'm the Orgy King." I watched as he walked up the road leaving duck-footed prints in the wet sand until he disappeared behind the jetty.

My neighbor Dave and his brother had covered my route while I was in Indiana. We met at Pete's Bake Shop the next morning at daybreak for the last time; he was quitting the Union Tribune. I recreated yesterday's bizarre scene at the Flood Control lagoon; an odd-looking stranger in cutoffs floating like an alligator amidst flotsam in an electrical storm who identified himself as the Orgy King. We had a good laugh, then parted ways. From the bakery I rode my bike to Sunset Cliffs to do my usual morning surf check.

There was a pocket beach at the foot of Pescadero Avenue, about a half-mile from the bakery. Unlike the sand bottom beach breaks, the bottom here was sandstone. The shape and character of the waves stayed pretty much the same year in and year out. A path led down the steep cliff to the beach below. About halfway down was a landing perfect for a surf check. On this morning the surf was flat and the sea surface glassy. The Sunset Cliffs surf spots required some size and a lower tide to come to life, but there was always something to ride at the beach on even the smallest days. Today would be a beach day. I pedaled back to the foot of Newport Avenue and found nicely formed small waves with a handful of guys out. Something up the beach caught my eye; it was the unmistakable profile of the Orgy King. He was sitting alone in his cutoffs staring out to sea. I needed to get my board and get in the water before the late morning wind set in. I wondered aloud as I pedaled away; "Who is that guy?"

The early surf culture was new and interesting. The community of local surfers was small and tightknit. The older guys had been at this for a few years. They all had nicknames like Mouse, Blackie, Root, Lizard, Rug, and so on. They explored the isolated breaks along Point Loma's Sunset Cliffs and attached names to the best of them. When I came on the scene all local surfers knew the location and characteristics of Newbreak, Ab, Sub, Garbage, Luscombs, Birdshit and Osprey, to name a few.

Local pioneer groups like this could be found in the beach communities from the Mexican Border to Santa Barbara. The only problem some days was finding someone to surf with. Just a few years later a writer in Hollywood would chronicle the adventures of his daughter at Malibu in a book titled *Gidget*. The blissful era of uncrowded waves was over.

OB Root, Mouse Robb and Crew at Garbage

I was soon back at South Beach and in the water. I paddled to my favorite spot off the rocks where the beach ends and the cliffs begin. In the late summer waves hit the coast from the south at a pronounced angle producing left breaking wave faces. On bigger days the longest rides at the beach began off the rocks and ended in front of the lifeguard station over a hundred yards away. I was a Goofy foot, which is kind of like being a southpaw. I face the wave going left and control the board with my left foot. The name derives from a 1937 Disney cartoon featuring Goofy surfing Hawaii for the first time wherein he stands with his right foot forward and repeatedly gets his ass handed to him.

I managed to catch a handful of small waves before a stiff wind ruined it. I exited the water and spotted the Orgy King sitting at a new location further up the beach. There was a girl sitting next to him that I recognized as Carol Wood, a beach girl and classmate whose father owned a business on Newport. I made a mental note to talk to Carol; I had to be on my way. It was the time of month I hated the most; I had to start collecting money from my paper customers in person, door to door.

The San Diego Union Tribune's arrangement with its paper carriers was diabolical. I was considered a contractor and was provided with the papers I delivered to their customers. Near the end of the month I got a bill for the papers. Any money I had left over was mine to keep. The best I could do if everybody paid up was forty dollars for the month. Folding and delivery took an average of three hours; more if it was raining and I had to wrap the deliveries in wax paper. Sundays took four hours or more. The carriers who delivered the evening paper had Sundays off. I had to make their customers' deliveries in addition to my own. The papers were the biggest and heaviest of the week by far. The manager who brought the papers to us would spot stacks of papers at locations along the route where I would wrap and reload my bags. I worked 106 hours a month delivering, plus 10 hours collecting. That came out to 35 cents an hour if everyone payed up, but that usually wasn't the case. Most of the time I netted much less. Several times in my paperboy career I had to borrow money to pay the bill.

I knew this would be a bad month. Most of my deliveries were to apartments and courts. At the end of summer there was always a flurry of moveouts. Maybe one in ten made good on their bill; the rest stiffed me. I had worked my way down Santa Monica Avenue to the lifeguard tower by early afternoon and it was not going well. I took a break and walked back over to Newport to Paco's Tacos. At Paco's five crispy rolled tacos smothered in guacamole and cheese could be had for twenty-five cents. I picked up my order at the window and took a seat in the small outdoor eating area.

I had been warned by John and others to avoid a local surfer named Rod Miller. He had the reputation of being a consummate asshole. He was approaching my table now with two followers in tow; one tall and creepy looking, the other scrawny and freckled. Miller stopped in front of my table, grinning from ear to ear. "Hey man how's it goin'? We're surfed out from this morning and we're all starving. Could you loan us a buck and a half until tomorrow?" I kept munching away on my last rolled taco. I had over fifty dollars in small bills and loose change in my pockets. I produced a one and two quarters and handed them to Miller. They rushed to the window to order. I swallowed my last bite and left to resume collection. I was almost out of earshot when I heard Miller and his gang laughing hysterically about something. It was Miller who loudly concluded; "What a dumbass!" Well, I had been warned.

I continued my collections feeling peeved with myself. Since I was four years old, I had witnessed frequent bloody violence at home and avoided confrontation, even in situations where it was warranted. I had already learned it was wise in the long run to just let it go but longed to deliver a well-deserved ass whupping to the likes of Rod Miller.

I finished my collections late that afternoon and went to the seawall at the end of Newport before going home. Carol had walked down from her father's shop for an evening swim and was coming out of the water headed my way. I called her over and asked her what she knew about the Orgy King. She told me his name was Ken Neal and he was indeed new to Ocean Beach. She had seen him sitting alone and stopped to introduce herself. She described him as polite and well spoken; not at all the nutcase I had imagined. He lived with his mother two blocks from the beach, near me. Carol said goodbye and moved on to get out of the chilly wind; I started home to count my money and pay my bill. Later that night the bill was paid with eighteen dollars and fifty cents left over.

I ran into John and his buddies at the fishing hole the next day; I told them about yesterday's encounter with Miller and his gang. I got a well-deserved "I told you so!" John went on to identify the two sidekicks: The scrawny freckled kid was Bobby Price, a neighbor; the tall sidekick was Bart Walters, a creepy guy who loved guns. John and Bobby were friends before Miller came along. It was Bobby who told John about Walters' love of guns and his hobby of killing seagulls. John told the story:

Bobby was invited over to go along on an evening hunt. Bart had a semi-automatic .22 caliber carbine he kept under his bed. He would leave for his hunts a few minutes before dusk. Bart preferred inclement weather and high tides when no one would be at the tidepools. He placed the stock of the loaded carbine under his armpit and donned a pullover hooded sweatshirt leaving only a couple inches of barrel protruding from his sleeve. He then walked the short distance to the cliffs and took his position on a ledge 10 feet below the top of the bluff and 20 feet above the tidepools. Gulls were numerous and took advantage of the updraft to soar along the cliffs. They streamed by the shooting perch from both directions at eye level creating a carnival shooting gallery. Bart had become an expert marksman and went for head shots that killed the gull instantly and sent it tumbling into the wave-washed tidepools below. Wounded gulls fell to the sandstone flapping and screeching. They were quickly silenced by a point-blank coup de grace. Bart slid down the pickle weed slope to the top of the seawall to finish the killing. Bobby had mentioned being creeped out by the satisfied grin on Bart's face when he crawled back up the pickleweed after an execution.

John continued: It was Bart who taught the Miller gang how to turpentine dogs. They would hunt around the neighborhood until they found a stray dog without an owner in sight. They brought cheese and hamburger to lure the pooch close enough to grab. Once they got their hands on the dog everyone worked to hold it still. Bart then raised the tail and applied turpentine. If the dog was a male, he produced a can of bright red spray paint from another pocket and applied a generous coat to the poor pooch's scrotum. The burning pain sent the dog into a frenzy; dragging its butt on the ground and crying loudly with red balls flopping. Miller's gang wallowed in an orgy of sadistic pleasure until the terrified dog ran off.

Miller and his gang picked on anyone who was different. Everyone in the neighborhood knew a local eccentric named Jimmy Marudas. Jimmy was fascinated with television antennas and spent his days wandering the alleys of Ocean Beach searching for components that had been tossed out. I saw him all the time; walking beside his bicycle bearing a heap of antenna parts. It was rumored all the stuff ended up in his backyard, in a TV antenna junkyard piled high with his treasure.

Jimmy also lived on Voltaire Street. He was a bit of an oddball but was friendly and harmless, and generally well-liked. For Miller and his gang Jimmy was low hanging fruit, and they delighted in pestering him. Also, there was a long-time OB resident who had been a polio victim and walked on a built-up shoe. I saw her almost daily walking along Cable Street on her way to or from Newport. She too was mocked and pestered mercilessly by Miller. He walked a block behind mimicking her clumsy gait to the amusement of his gang. It was only a matter of time until the roving band of hyenas found fresh meat in the form of our latest unconventional newcomer; the Orgy King.

3 BASSLIPS MCLAREN

Flood Control Opaleye

I got a surprise visit from my cousin Dennis on vacation from Indiana. He had two days free before moving on to San Francisco. I took Dennis for an afternoon of fishing. I showed him how to rig for Opaleye; a single hook on four feet of leader below a cork bobber. It was mid-afternoon when we tossed our fresh razor clams into the still waters of the Flood Control lagoon. Off to our left was a friendly old lady who was a regular at the fishing hole. She had taught me how to catch the abundant feisty green Opaleye when we first met. I smiled and waved to her and she waved back. She held up three fingers to tell me she had fish on the stringer.

An approaching car with a rotted-out muffler shattered the peace. Down the dirt road came McLaren in his smoking rusted beater. He drove out to the old coots' honey hole on the point. He emerged from the car with a Pall Mall dangling from his enormous lips followed by blowing tufts of upholstery stuffing. He wore the same stained undershirt that struggled in vain to cover his enormous belly. He spotted the old lady sitting on the other side of Dennis and me. He waved and shouted across the lagoon; "Jean how the hell are you?" The lady rose to her feet, lifted a middle finger high above her head and shouted back; "Kiss my ass McLaren! Go to hell and take that piece of shit car with you!" He grabbed his belly and laughed, got back in his rusty beater and drove back up the dirt road to town. Dennis muttered aloud what we were both thinking; "What the hell was that all about?"

I went over to Jean and formally introduced myself for the first time. Jean was crusty, talkative, and funny. She had lived in Ocean Beach for 10 years. Her husband passed away 3 years ago at the age of 68; she was 65. She and her husband were regular patrons at the Arizona, a bowling alley bar on Bacon Street.

Not too long after Jean's husband died, McLaren approached her at the bar. He offered to bring her fresh fish fillets any time, free of charge. Jean loved seafood and gladly accepted his offer. The free fish was just a ruse to get her alone in her house. McLaren showed up with a dead Sand Bass the following day. Once he was inside and the front door closed, he forced himself on Jean who promptly kicked him square in the balls and punched him in the throat. He ran from the house bent over in pain and struggling to breathe.

Jean said he persisted, hitting on her again and again in vain. McLaren fancied himself a Swordsman specializing in single ladies and widows between 65 and 80 years of age. His lead-in move was always an offer of fresh fish fillets. Now it was abundantly clear why he was so territorial about the lagoon honey hole; the Sand Bass was his ticket to ride. I would later hear stories identical to Jean's. The scheme apparently worked well enough to keep him supplied with an adequate supply of geriatric nookie.

We said goodbye to Jean and headed back to my place to clean our catch. From the top of the jetty we spotted a commotion taking place in the middle of the street by A-1 Bait & Tackle; Rod's pack had found the Orgy King. They had surrounded him and were taunting him with something. Dennis and I agreed without speaking; we had to do something. We put down our rods and stringer of fish at the base of the jetty and strode to the scene. As we drew closer, we could see that the gang had snatched a fountain pen that the King desperately wanted back. It was clear Rod had pulled some shit to goad him into a lopsided fight. We walked into the pack without breaking stride. Dennis stepped in front of Walters and gave him a shove backwards that nearly knocked him over. Bobby Price was there, along with a fourth guy who promptly ran off down West Point Loma Boulevard. Dennis was formidable; tall and stocky. Bobby Price indicated with upraised hands that he wanted no part of what was about to happen.

Dennis advanced on Walters with fists raised. Rod Miller stepped forward to punch him from behind. Before I could react, the King's big hand grabbed Rod by the hair and yanked him backwards away from Dennis. Rod stumbled backward to keep from falling over. The King hopped alongside to keep him from falling, and to build momentum, then planted his feet and forcefully slammed the stumbling Miller headfirst into the door of a Helms Bakery truck. The King descended on the semi-conscious Miller, raining blows onto his head and upper body. I was afraid he was going to kill him; I stepped forward and hooked his arm in mid swing.

It was all over in a few seconds. Walters stayed off at a safe distance in silence, expressionless with his eyes hidden behind sunglasses. Bobby, assisted by the Helms Bakery driver, knelt to check on Miller who was on the ground and out cold. I reached down and picked up the King's fountain pen and handed it to him. We left Bobby, Walters, and the Helms man to deal with Rod. The King came with us to the jetty where we had left our gear. We heard approaching sirens; a small crowd had gathered around Miller. We feared the authorities would soon be looking for us. My nearby cave under the boulders was an ideal hiding place.

It was a tight fit with Dennis and the sizeable King. I had a rush of claustrophobia. I had always been leery of caves going back to my earliest days in Indiana where limestone caves were abundant. My cousins enjoyed exploring the cave systems. I wanted no part of it and never went beyond the opening.

Outside the sirens grew near then fell silent, then came the crackle of police radios. Dennis muttered our shared fear aloud; "God I hope you didn't kill him!" A wave of dread swept over us. I pulled the playing cards from their hiding place and showed them to the others. The grainy images of everyone's Aunt Mabel banging a guy in shiny black shoes passed the time and brought forth some nervous laughter. My imagination was running wild now; we could be arrested for murder and sentenced to prison. My family couldn't afford to have this happen; there was no safety net. We sat in nervous claustrophobic silence for what seemed like forever. Eventually, it occurred to me that it had been quiet outside for a while. I crawled over and peeked out through an opening; everyone was gone except for a single police car parked at the curb. The cop was writing something down and talking on his radio. After a few minutes he drove off toward Newport Avenue.

Relieved for the moment, we crawled out of the cave and over the jetty rocks to the Flood Control side. In the distance the old coots were working the honey hole on the point. The King spotted a familiar figure sitting on a ripped-up dining room chair waiting for a bite. "Gawd, it's McLaren. What a frickin' asshole!" At that point I introduced myself and asked him to elaborate on the mysterious McLaren. The Orgy King was indeed Ken Neal and was new to town just as Carol had said. Now I wanted to know; who was this fat old guy in the stained undershirt that everyone seemed to know and despise? Come to find out, Ken knew him personally. We were all ears as Ken told his story:

Ken was adopted. He lived in an apartment in the same block of Brighton as Jean the fisher lady. His elderly mother's name was Birdie. Birdie passed her time sitting in a chair with a TV tray in front of her drinking hard liquor from a water glass. When drunk, which was often, she became belligerent and combative. Ken and his mom had gotten a lucky break recently when the owner of their apartment complex hired them to manage the rental units. This meant free rent along with some monthly income to supplement Birdie's Social Security. Ken went out that day to search the Newport thrift shops for clothing suitable for his new role of Landlord. He found his idea of the perfect Landlord outfit: a top hat, ascot, and walking stick to go with his corduroy blazer. By the time Ken returned home that afternoon, the Neals had been fired and evicted. Birdie had gotten baked early and picked a fight with her neighbors. The neighbors called the building owner who walked into an inebriated buzz saw. It was a short conflagration that concluded with her being fired and ordered off the property.

Birdie was on McLaren's hit list. He had been busy laying the groundwork for a score and had been in Ken's house to soften the target with fresh fish. He traded his filthy tee shirt for an XXXL Hawaiian unbuttoned halfway down exposing a rug of chest hair. Gold chains hung from his fat neck and lay tangled in the rug. He reeked of Old Spice cologne and fish. Here and there in the thick black hair covering his arms an occasional fish scale glinted. His black hair was slicked back, held in place by a handful of Pomade. As with his arms, fish scales here and there glittered in the sunlight. Before he could taste Birdie's delights, he had to get Ken out of the house.

McLaren showed up one day with great news; he had found a paying job for Ken working on a boat. He even offered to pick him up and bring him home, so Ken didn't have to spend money on the bus. The next day the smoking beater pulled up in front of Ken's complex at eight, sharp. McLaren drove to a downtrodden dock complex in the harbor's Commercial Basin. It was a graveyard of inoperable, rotting fishing boats whose proud days at sea were long gone. Ken's job was to muck out the bilge of a scow McLaren apparently had some interest in. It listed heavily to port and was covered in seagull crap. The wheelhouse windows had all been busted out by vandals. All the commercial fishing gear on the deck and navigational equipment in the wheelhouse had been stolen. The bilge was a petri dish of stinking mystery fluid that had been fermenting there in the dark for years. McLaren was eager to get on with his seduction and left Ken to his task. Ken waded into the viscous goo in his cutoffs and began taking it up top to throw overboard one bucket at a time. All the toilets in San Diego flushed into San Diego Bay at that time; the bay was where boaters and businesses tossed their empty paint cans and used motor oil. No one would look twice at the foul slick that soon covered the water around the scow.

After six hours of bucketing the floor of the bilge was still wet but visible. The sound of a muffler-less car in the distance alerted Ken that his ride home had arrived. McLaren came down the ramp from the parking lot in a huff. He had a bandage wrapped around his head and one puffy eye. He was in a foul mood when he lifted the hatch to look at the bilge. He was not satisfied with the job Ken had done and was pissed. Ken got his ass chewed then rode home in icy silence. McLaren finally spoke as Ken exited the car; "You're fired!"

Ken went into his unit and found his inebriated mom in her chair asleep and snoring. The place was a mess; it looked like there had been a struggle that had gone room to room before ending near the front door. In the middle of the living room floor was a cast iron frying pan; a few feet away lay a soiled butcher knife. Broken glass from falling pictures covered the floor at the base of the walls.

After dropping Ken off at the boat that morning, McLaren had gone to the honey hole to toss a line and update the coots on his unfolding conquest. He then went home to gussy up and slap on a bottle of cologne. McLaren's error in timing was a near-fatal miscalculation. In the three hours all this took, Birdie was getting plastered. When he finally arrived fish fillets in hand the possibly cooperative target had morphed again into an inebriated buzz saw. Just what went down was not clear, but the way it ended was: One or more blows to the head with a cast iron skillet and a stab wound to the groin.

Ken was a superb storyteller; purveyor of low comedy at its best. He related the tragic story of his alcoholic mom and her unscrupulous senior suitor through a filter of dark humor; we were crying tears of laughter when his story concluded. Out of the chaotic day came a new friend.

Ken bore an uncanny resemblance to someone; I couldn't remember who. I studied his face as he was telling his story, trying to remember. Just before we parted to go our separate ways it dawned on me: On the counter at Liticker's there was a display advertising Trader Vic's Hot Buttered Rum mix; it had been there for ages. Ken was a younger version of the Trader Vic portrayed on the jar. I asked; "Has anyone ever told you that you look like Trader Vic the rum guy?" Nicknames were big then; we all had one. The name stuck; Ken was no longer the Orgy King, nor was he Ken; he was Trader Vic now. In the coming weeks he would be introduced to my crew as Trader Vic; many would never know his real name.

Kenneth "Trader Vic" Neal

I saw Rod Miller several days later; he was sitting by himself at the seawall staring out to sea with one arm in a sling and wearing a neck brace. He had gotten no satisfaction from the police; eyewitnesses on the scene all agreed it was Miller who was the aggressor. His gang deserted him in the days following his beating. Left on his own, he was still a prick but no longer a significant prick.

4 TALES FROM THE BAT CAVE

Bali Hai Tiki

The family moved to a small house on Brighton Avenue that had a huge backyard and a two-room granny flat out back. I got the granny flat all to myself; it quickly became a hangout for my friends who dubbed it "The Bat Cave". The two-room flat was situated under a huge Torrey Pine and had only one window. It was always cool and dark, and I loved it. I lived closest to the beach of my surfing friends, most of whom didn't drive yet, so I soon had a quiver of longboards lining the fence in back of the flat.

The Brighton house had been owned by an eccentric artist who made his living carving tikis from palm tree logs. Polynesian themes were popular at that time, and the new waterfront dinner houses and hotels going in on Shelter Island generated a big demand for his carvings. He was also a pioneer surfer who shaped custom balsawood surfboards. For reasons unknown, he left in a hurry leaving several unfinished tikis scattered about the property. In the Bat Cave attic, he left a hidden pint of Bacardi rum. I did not yet drink alcohol, but kept it for some future special occasion, nonetheless.

Under the house I found a mint condition balsa longboard that was left behind. In the side yard under the Torrey Pine was a beautiful lapstrake surf dory also left behind. It appeared to have been there for a long time. I bought a few cans of marine caulk and started the tedious job of sealing the cracks between the strakes. On wet winter days when the surf was no good, I spent my time working on the dory. I had no idea how I was going to get it to the water. It was about twenty feet in length and weighed a ton.

I bought my first car for forty dollars from an elderly neighbor; a 1936 Ford Sedan Delivery panel truck he had purchased new for his gardening business. It was an illegal deathtrap that required a team to drive. There were no brake lights, so one guy laid on the floor of the truck with the rear door ajar. He had a flashlight covered with red cellophane which he activated when I yelled "brakes". The brakes were mechanical; outlawed years ago after hydraulic brakes were invented. The ancient brakes would barely bring the panel truck to a stop. If we had to stop on an incline, two other crew members stood ready to fling open the rear cargo door and passenger door and drag their feet if needed. Also, I didn't have a driver's license.

1936 Ford Sedan Delivery Deathtrap

We avoided driving after dark. We found out early on that the generator didn't put out enough juice to power the headlights and fire the plugs simultaneously. Night driving required a headlight man to scan the road ahead for cops. We ran dark until he spotted anything that looked like a police car, then pulled out the dash headlight knob causing the motor to sputter until the danger passed and the headlights turned off again.

We got bold after months of driving in daylight to and

from the beach unmolested. On a cold night in February Trader and I decided to go shark fishing in Mission Bay. We rounded up a flight crew: Bat Cave regulars "Mouse" Marions, "Swabby" Johnson, and "Tinman" Tinsley.

There was an older Mouse in Ocean Beach, legendary lifeguard and pioneer surfer Jim Robb who derived his name from his diminutive stature. Garry "Mouse" Marions, on the other hand, actually looked like a rodent; buck teeth, big ears, and pointy nose minus the whiskers. Don Johnson derived his nickname from his love of Naval Speedos, the bun-hugging swim trunks the rest of us wouldn't be caught dead in.

We put fifty cents worth of regular gas in the tank and set off for Quivira Basin at sunset loaded with fishing rods. It was never intended to be a night of mayhem and vandalism but that's the way it turned out. We set up shop next to the Seaforth Sportfishing landing. The area was lit up by dim overhead lights, which made it easier to see. The lights also drew fish to the nearby docks.

After an hour of unproductive fishing, someone suggested we borrow a landing utility boat. In those days, docks were not gated, and outbuildings not locked. We found an aluminum rowboat at the base of the ramp; now all we needed was a set of oars which we found in the dock boathouse. The destination was the bait receiver anchored in the middle of Quivira Basin; a dependable hot spot any time of year. Mouse, along with crew members Tinman and the Swabby rowed out into the blackness to give it a go.

Trader and I stayed behind to man the base of operations. We were getting very hungry; no one had thought to bring food. In the landing breezeway were five coin-operated gumball machines, one of which was loaded with cashews. We turned our pockets inside out looking for nickels to no avail. I gave up and returned to my fishing spot. A short time later the sound of breaking glass from the breezeway signaled an end to Trader's patience. I returned to find him on all fours harvesting nuts from the glittering field of splintered glass; a large rock lay on the ground under the vending machines. I joined in; soon we had filled our jacket pockets with delicious cashews and splintered glass.

A short time later, the rowboat crew appeared out of the dark with an enormous Leopard Shark from the bait barge. It was the biggest fish Mouse had ever caught, and he was going to take it home to show off. We shared our purloined bounty with the others and started packing up. It was approaching three in the morning; it was time to go home. We loaded our gear and Mouse's trophy shark. Everyone manned their duty stations in the truck, and we were off.

We went about three hundred yards before the truck sputtered and died; we had run out of gas. We walked back to the sportfishing landing to rummage for gas in the boat house. We found no gas but did find an empty steel container. At the curb in front of the landing was an unoccupied Porsche 911. We cut a length of hose from the ramp washdown bib and proceeded to attempt to siphon a container full of gas from the Porsche. We each took a turn trying to suck some gas up the hose and into our steel container to no avail. It was our last hope; we were going to have to walk home.

We started back in the direction of the truck; it was dark and freezing cold. In the distance we saw two figures approaching. As they drew closer, I could see it was a couple in formal attire. We met under the dim light of a streetlamp. The young woman's hair was disheveled; she smelled of alcohol. She was struggling to walk in her stiletto heels that were visible below her stained evening gown. The man's tuxedo was frumpy and disorganized; his black tie hung from one side of his neck, his cummerbund had come undone and dragged behind him like a tail. He too reeked of alcohol. In one hand he held a length of hose, in the other a gas can. That explained why we couldn't get anything out of the Porsche; it was out of gas too. Like us, the couple spotted a nearby vehicle and got out the siphoning gear. The irony of the situation spawned a smattering of hoarse laughter, then we both moved on without a word.

I biked over the bridge to retrieve the panel truck the next afternoon. A motorcycle cop was in the process of writing a parking ticket when I arrived on the scene. "Is this your truck?" he inquired. I blurted out before thinking; "Yes sir, it's mine." I should have just left it there; the truck wasn't registered, I had no insurance, and no driver's license. It took the cop a half hour to write up the twenty-one equipment violations. About half-way through he called two other cops to the scene to enjoy the bust; I had apparently set a record for equipment violations on a single vehicle. The stench of Mouse's rotting Leopard Shark completed the scene.

The cops chuckled and shook their heads, but in the end were sympathetic to my situation. The motorcycle cop suggested I get rid of the truck before the two-week deadline for fixing the violations; it was obvious I could not afford the repairs. An older guy in Point Loma had been after me for months to sell the truck. He and his son did full restorations of classic cars for a hobby. I sold the 1936 Ford Sedan Delivery for forty dollars the same day. The citing officer, old enough to be my father, scolded me before tearing up the ticket for driving without a license.

I had heard it said that when one door closes, another opens. A week later I was on a weekend trip to the backcountry with friends when I found my dream car. It was sitting in a vacant field outside of Ramona with a For Sale sign on the windshield; "Runs, Everything Works, $150 Firm." We stopped and looked it over. The next day I was back with the money. I drove my prize back to OB and parked it in front of the Brighton house. Mouse had a newer Ford that he let me use to take my driver's test. After one failed attempt, I was finally legit; a solid car and valid California Driver's License.

1950 Ford Country Squire Woody

Among my tribe of Bat Cave friends were several large guys; Mouse, Trader, and myself included. Gordy Newton and his brother Ken, Dwight Lobb, and John Bishop rounded out the Half Ton Boys. We were all sitting around on the beach one day when someone, for some reason, added up our combined weight which came to one thousand one hundred twenty pounds; one-half a long ton. "Half Long-Ton Boys" was too awkward so we went with "Half Ton Boys".

I had an epiphany one summer morning as I was finishing the dory; I didn't need a truck and trailer to float the dory. We had enough muscle to physically carry the boat to the Flood Control for a christening. On a hot summer day in mid-July the Half Ton Boys showed up for the big event. We hoisted the dory aloft and carried it down the middle of Brighton to North Beach, then to the dirt road leading to the Flood Control.

I don't know why, but I wasn't yet familiar with wood's tendency to swell when wet and shrink when dry. I had spent hours sealing the lapstrake hull in the rainy months of winter. It was mid-summer now and the hull was bone dry. We slipped the dory into the water; it was a beautiful sight worth all the effort I had put into it. One by one we shoehorned into the dory and started rowing toward the Sunset Cliffs bridge a half-mile up the river. All went well for the first few minutes, then the first little geyser sprayed up from a crack below the water line, then another. Within minutes water was pouring into the boat through a multitude of cracks. Near the middle of the river, in twenty feet of water, the dory sank to the bottom like a stone. We all treaded water in silent disbelief for a while, then started the swim to shore. For the next few years I visited the wreck while snorkeling. The boat quickly became a reef that attracted fish and other life. Over the years it was a great place to spearfish until finally disappearing beneath the river sediment forever.

Half tonner John Bishop showed up at the beach several days after the dory disaster excited about his new job; he was hired as a deckhand aboard the *Smoky Stover,* a water taxi that ferried fishermen to and from an offshore fishing barge. Earlier that year an enterprising partnership had anchored the *California,* a derelict 130-foot barge, three miles off Ocean Beach. The *California* was outfitted with live bait tanks, seating, a tackle shop, and a small eatery serving hamburgers, hotdogs, and bags of chips. For five bucks you could fish from dawn until dusk and beyond. The *Smoky Stover* made regular runs to and from the barge during daylight hours. John invited us to come and check it out; the Swabby and I took him up on it.

Fishing Barge California

We boarded the *Smoky Stover* at dawn the following morning. The boat was a painfully slow single diesel that belched clouds of black smoke from its single stack. The *California* came into view a few minutes after rounding the south jetty. It looked old, a ghost of what was once a proud seagoing ship, stripped down and decayed but still afloat. The skipper pulled alongside the barge and John made fast to a small landing long enough for us to jump off. We reached the main deck, put down our gear, and went for a stroll around the deck where a dozen or so fishermen were hard at it. There was a wide-open Bonito bite going on; it was going to be a fun morning of fishing. We ordered a couple of egg sandwiches from the galley and claimed a spot on the rail facing south with a view of the Los Coronados Islands in Mexico.

I tossed out a live anchovy under a homemade broom handle bobber and unwrapped my egg sandwich and chips. I was munching away when the unmistakable smell of burning marijuana reached my nose. I looked to the far end of the boat where a couple was huddled together smoking a joint. A moment later came the pungent scent Patchouli Oil wafting on the breeze. The couple didn't appear to be fishing; they apparently came out to get stoned in a picturesque and safe place. The pot laws were harsh; a roach in the ashtray of your car would get you arrested and imprisoned. Getting caught with an ounce or more could put you away for a long time.

My broom handle bobber suddenly ripped sideways and disappeared below the waves; line peeled off the reel as the fish made a sustained first run, then sounded and dug in deep; a sure sign I had a Yellowtail on. Bonito and Barracuda were the mainstays of the Barge fishery; Yellowtail were highly sought after but seldom caught. We soon had a crowd of curious onlookers around us, including the stoner couple from the far end of the boat. After a brief game of tug o' war I could finally see colors; I sent Swabby Don to fetch a gaff. We boated a beautiful iridescent medium-size Yellow a short time later; everyone gathered around to get a closer look.

A familiar voice in the crowd of onlookers offered congratulations; "Nice fish man…really cool colors!" I looked up to see who had made the comment; my jaw dropped; it was Soupy Sales, star of my favorite TV show. He and his girlfriend were the couple getting stoned at the far end of the boat. I was star-struck; I sputtered out a "thank you". Most of the other fishermen didn't realize we had a celebrity in our midst. The few who did brought anything that could be written on for an autograph. Soupy was gracious and funny, signing autographs and making White Fang noises.

The *Smoky Stover* pulled alongside to pick up passengers for the shuttle back to Mission Bay. Soupy and his girlfriend started for the landing to board the shuttle; I raced to the landing with a piece of crumpled notebook paper for a last- minute autograph. A handful of fans lined the rail and waved farewell as the *Smoky Stover* belched a ball of black diesel smoke and chugged off toward the harbor. That evening we pulled in a *Lunch with Soupy* rerun on Channel 5 out of Los Angeles. I had an old black and white TV hooked to rabbit ears with tinfoil extensions; the picture was snowy, and the sound was awful, but it didn't matter.

5 PESCADERO TRAGEDY

The Giant Dipper Belmont Park

I spent a lot of time caring for Donna, Jerry and Garry; my younger siblings. My woody was a familiar sight around OB; me behind the wheel, Trader Vic riding shotgun, and three little heads bobbing in the rear windows. We regularly trekked over the bridges to Mission Beach to ride the Big Dipper roller coaster at Belmont Park. The kids were too small to ride and obediently stayed on a bench where I could see them from above. We loved the front car and usually got it. We rode until we ran out of money.

We were returning from Belmont Park one afternoon when Trader wanted to stop in the middle of the San Diego River bridge. I obliged and waited to see what was going to happen next; with Trader Vic you never knew. He exited the woody, closed the door, and promptly vaulted over the bridge railing. I drove to a dirt parking lot below the bridge and waited for him to swim to shore. He was fully clothed and soaking wet with mud up to his knees. We continued our drive home as if nothing had happened; it was a typical day with Trader Vic. He was a Superhero to the kids who thought he was invincible.

Danny Clouse was a guy almost as radical as Trader. They had become good friends. It wasn't long before the two of them were jumping off the bridge together every week. They soon discovered that the water under the bridge was very shallow and peak high tide was best time to jump. Even then they were pile driven feet first into the soft sediment up to their knees. When mere jumping was no longer exciting, they engaged in theatrics aimed at passing motorists. Danny would stand atop the bridge railing as if threatening suicide. Trader would feign pleading with him from the sidewalk below. Then, in full view of rubber necking motorists, Danny jumped. Screeching tires followed; frantic drivers and passengers went to the rail to peer over the edge. That's when they found out they'd been had. Danny would be treading water below, grinning ear to ear and laughing. They reversed roles each day with Trader being the diver and Danny the Good Samaritan. It was just a matter of time before they pissed off the wrong motorist.

It was Saturday. I was taking a nap after a morning surf at the Cliffs. The siblings were yelling to me that Trader was on TV. I stumbled into the room where the midday news was showing film from an earlier arrest that had taken place on the San Diego River bridge. There was Danny Clouse laying on the hood of a police car with his hands cuffed behind his back and a cop's hand gripping the back of his neck. A few feet away Trader was being interrogated by the police and City lifeguards. It turned out that there was no ordinance prohibiting jumping off the San Diego River bridge. After all, who in their right mind would jump off a bridge into water so shallow that at low tide it was basically just wet mud. The daredevils were cited for creating a public nuisance and swimming in an unauthorized area.

A few weeks later I took a bike ride to Mission Beach. When I crossed the San Diego river bridge it was a minus two-foot tide. I stopped at the center span and looked down. A rotted out hot water heater protruded from the mud directly below, its rusty torn metal edges in plain view. A shopping cart lay half buried in the mud a few feet away. A rusted automobile fender lay buried in the mud with its jagged curved edge exposed. The boys were lucky the law intervened before one or the other was shredded on the rusty junk below.

To replace the exhilaration of bridge jumping, Trader joined me in body surfing the high tide Pescadero shore break. The reefs quit breaking during high tides, delivering the full force of the swells right onto the beach in a hollow shore break. We delighted in body surfing the powerful waves that ended with a pounding on dry sand. It is a miracle none of us were killed or paralyzed. A crew of older guys partied on the beach almost every summer night. It was here, sitting around a bonfire, that we were introduced to Rainier Ale; the "Green Death". The cheap rotgut ale was the official Pescadero drink. I was goaded into trying a swig, then another, then another. I ended up sprawled out in a bed of pickleweed alongside an Orchard Avenue duplex with my feet in the air like I had tried to walk up the side of the building and failed; I didn't remember how I got there. The whole world was spinning, and I was about to puke my guts up.

Midway up the bluff behind Pescadero beach there was a natural indentation in the sandstone. Summer beachgoers would often sit on the shaded ledge to get out of the sun. The beach was wide in those days and stretched north to the foot of Del Mar Avenue. It was a favorite hangout for my group of locals; not as crowded as Ocean Beach, and more accessible than No Surf, the popular pocket beach further out on Sunset Cliffs. The waves here were slow and friendly most days and less crowded than other nearby spots.

The north and west swells of winter brought larger and more challenging waves to the reefs at Pescadero. With the summer crowds gone the few of us that stuck with it had the place all to ourselves. I went to the Pescadero landing during a late January north swell and found well-formed six-foot waves nicely groomed by an icy morning offshore wind. I scampered up the path to street level to change and grab my board. A short time later I was sitting outside waiting for waves. During a lull between sets, I looked to shore and spotted something odd on the bluff; someone had been digging to enlarge the natural indentation in the sandstone.

For the next two hours I traded waves with two others at the peak directly off the street-end. There was a little gang of Gremmies that showed up nearly every day at the same time. They were led by a tall Goofyfoot named Ray who had a penchant for ruining my best lefts by taking off in front me. By ten o'clock the Gremmies had arrived, and a cold north wind had set in. I paddled in and headed for the warmth of the car heater. I was almost to street level when I saw a familiar figure coming down the Orchard Avenue trail; it was John Finlay. It had been a long time since we had seen each other.

I slid my board into the wagon and went down to meet John on the beach. He approached me carrying a spade in one hand and comic books in the other. "What the hell are you doing?" I asked. "We're making a place to hang out." He replied. I voiced my disapproval; "You know these cliffs are dangerous as hell, right? You shouldn't be doing this!" John replied; "The neighbors around here have told us the same thing. We'll be fine." He turned to greet two other members of his work team coming down the Orchard path. They carried an assortment of tools and snack food. I had said my piece; I headed back up the path shaking my head and mumbling to myself.

I learned early on that Sunset Cliffs was a beautiful but dangerous place. It seemed that not a week went by without a rescue, injury, or fatality. Large surf combined with high tides were the worst. Multiple sirens headed south on Sunset Cliffs Boulevard almost always meant there was trouble at the Cliffs. Tourists and visitors who weren't familiar with the area were occasionally surprised by set waves and washed off the rocks into treacherous whirlpools. Bluff collapses were common; often not seen or heard. You just noticed one day while driving along the cliffs that something looked different. Upon closer examination it was a section of a familiar cliff face that had fallen into the sea in the dead of night.

Two days later the weather turned wet and blustery. It was a holiday Monday, Lincoln's birthday. I went to Pete's for morning Danish and coffee as usual. Rain was sheeting against the bakery's glass storefront; the palm trees along Newport were swaying and dropping fronds here and there. When I finished my breakfast the rain had stopped, and it was still. I drove out to Garbage for the morning surf check out of curiosity more than anything. It was a mess, and I was soon on my way home with a stop at the Pescadero landing. On my way down the path I heard a voice call out to me; it was John standing in the doorway of the cave with two of his buddies. He invited me to come in and see the completed project; I declined with a headshake and animated wave. I scrambled back up the path and headed home for a nap. I had been up until the wee hours of the morning with a painful ear infection, a common problem associated with being in the water every day.

I took an aspirin and stretched out in the Bat Cave for a snooze. I was awakened from a sound sleep by sirens. There were many of them and they seemed to be coming from all directions. I pulled a pillow over my head but that didn't work. Heavy emergency equipment rolling by on nearby Sunset Cliffs Boulevard shook the house; the sirens continued from all directions. I got up and went into the main house. Mom was working the holiday. My young siblings were being cared for by an elderly babysitter named Margaret. She was glued to the television watching a news bulletin. "What's going on?" I asked. "Some boys were buried in a cave at Sunset Cliffs an hour ago. They're still digging them out!"

"Oh, Jesus no!" I blurted out. I jumped into the wagon and headed back toward Pescadero. I drove to the top of the hill overlooking the scene. A swarm of emergency vehicles were clustered at the foot of Pescadero and Orchard Avenue. I saw City lifeguard rescue equipment, too many police cars to count, and several ambulances, all with their red roof lights spinning. A throng of onlookers was backed up behind the police lines all the way to Sunset Cliffs Boulevard and beyond. I parked and began walking down the hill to the scene. It was a ghastly sight; somewhere in the crowd near the police line a woman was shrieking; John's sister or mother I thought. I made my way to the end of Orchard and climbed up onto an apartment balcony. From there I could see a portion of the beach. A dozen or more men were digging furiously with shovels and bare hands. City lifeguards and medics were working on someone several feet away. All I could see was a pair of motionless dirty feet protruding from the cluster of rescuers.

I spotted a lifeguard coming up the Orchard path toward my location. I yelled out from the balcony as he passed below carrying a load of rescue gear; "What's the word?" He replied without looking up: "One dead on the beach, one on the way to the hospital, and one still buried". So, there was a glimmer of hope that John had survived. The rescuers had given up on the boy on the beach. I watched as they placed his body on a lifeguard stretcher and covered him with a tarp. Shortly thereafter I was chased off the balcony and had to go back into the growing crowd of curious onlookers arriving from all over the city. I walked back up the hill and sat in the car listening for bulletins on the local radio stations.

The full story was front page news in the Union newspaper the following morning: a total of five boys were in the cave at the time it collapsed. Two boys were sitting near the entrance when pieces of the roof began to fall; the one nearest the opening rolled clear of the falling dirt, the other was buried up to his waist but managed to free himself. The other three, including John, were deep in the cave and had no chance to escape.

John Finlay Jr.

6 MA KELLOGG

Jean "Ma" Kellogg

Ma Kellogg was barely five feet tall and heavy-set. Her standard attire was a floral print muumuu and flip flops. She wore her hair straight and close cropped. Ma took crap from no one; she was a force to be reckoned with. Ma Kellogg was like a den mother to our tribe. The Kellogg house on Niagara Avenue in upper OB was our home away from home. It was a safe zone where Sheriff Jean Kellogg was the law.

Once you proved yourself worthy, Ma would let you drink beer so long as you behaved. Most of us were underage and had to observe Ma's rules lest we lose our valued membership in the club. None of us were regular drinkers but we loved to party, especially on warm summer evenings after being in the ocean all day. On keg nights Ma would provide the beer and sometimes snacks. She was always on the lookout for overindulgence and took your mug away when she sensed you'd had enough. No one could leave the property until Ma looked you over. On the rare occasions when someone needed a designated driver, our squeaky-clean Mouse was the go-to guy.

Ma's middle son Gale was one of the surf crew and good friends with my frequent diving and surfing partner, Kenji Kozuma. Gale surfed, devoured science fiction novels, and played the drums as did his brothers. Gerry Kozuma was Kenji's sister, and a fellow member of Ma Kellogg's flock. She had a marvelous voice she shared with us when the late-night guitars came out. Most of us had girlfriends who Ma knew and loved as well. Leslie was Gale's girl and part of the Kellogg family. Frankie was Kenji's steady and one of the prettiest girls in her class. Frankie's father did not approve of his daughter dating a Japanese boy. On the night of Frankie's prom, I was forced to squeeze into Kenji's small tuxedo for the pickup. The sleeves came to just below my elbows; the pant legs didn't reach my ankles. I arranged the cummerbund to hide my unbuttoned trousers.

The ongoing revelry at Ma's place did not go unnoticed by the neighbors. Music had begun to play a major part in our lives; there was a garage jam session every time we got together. All but one neighbor tolerated the racket; a few even came to the garage to listen. Mr. Martin, a neighbor who lived across the street, had complained from day one about our presence in the neighborhood. He painted the picture, for all who would listen, of randy surf bums who would never work a day in their lives, that drove loud beat up cars, and were probably on drugs. Ironically his stepson Tom was one of us.

We took every opportunity to discreetly pester Mr. Martin. After we learned he was annoyed by our music, we turned up the volume. Instead of parking our cars in the alley behind Ma's garage, we began parking bumper to bumper on the street, directly in front of his house. Someone, we don't know who, requisitioned a rotting Marlin head from the Point Loma Seafoods gut cans and placed it in Mr. Martin's toilet while he was at work. That sent him over the edge; Ma told us to cool it, which we did. Ma was taking incoming crap on a regular basis. We were aware that she could be in trouble if the police became involved. We extended the olive branch; we changed our ways; the band even turned down the volume a little bit.

This was the era of the Garage Band. In a garage a few blocks away from Ma's our friends Hugh McIntosh and Rob Winsett formed the Comancheros. The Impalas was another excellent OB band whose drummer, Paul Bleifuss, would later join our band, the Inmates, after Gale was drafted into the Army.

The Inmates

Standing: Steve & Kenji   Seated: Gale & Tom

I was a fledgling guitarist, Kenji had a saxophone, and Tom was an aspiring bass player. The whole thing got started because Gale had a full acoustic drum kit set up in the garage where he and his brothers practiced. Willie, Gales older brother, was well known in local music circles. Over time our amateurish jam sessions began to tighten up. A neighbor lady came over to listen one night; she was an event planner with Sacred Heart Catholic Church. After listening to a few surf instrumentals, she offered us a paying gig. We were all taken aback; we never figured people would pay to hear us; we were just having fun in the garage.

Two weeks later, on an October harvest moon night, we boarded the ferry boat *Murietta* at the Broadway Pier in downtown San Diego. There was a space amidships in front of the bar reserved for our setup. We were totally unprepared to play a four-hour gig. Gerry Kozuma was our only vocalist. Surf music was popular then and we knew them all. Our meager song list consisted of forty-five minutes of music which we would repeat throughout the night. The bar next to our makeshift stage had every flavor of hard liquor imaginable. All popular brands of beer were available from tubs of ice. Two bartenders in black tie attire readied for a busy evening. This was astounding to me; I was from a Baptist family. Catholics had a far different take on alcohol. It would be an interesting night.

We were a half-hour overdue to set sail. I learned that the *Murietta* would not leave the dock, nor would the bar open, until blessed by Monsignor Dillon who was running late. The passengers were getting impatient and thirsty. The Monsignor finally arrived. He didn't come aboard, but gave his blessing, exchanged pleasantries with the congregation, and left to return to Sacred

Heart. The bar was immediately mobbed by the parched parishioners. The ferry crew cast off the lines, and the cruise was underway.

Gerry Kozuma

We had never performed in public before. We made several nervous mistakes then settled into a comfortable groove. The tiny dance floor between us and the bar was quickly filled to capacity. It was a new and exciting experience; people having fun and responding to our music. We kept recycling our twelve or so songs throughout the night; the joyous and inebriated crowd never noticed or cared. The skipper took us to the mouth of the bay then came about for the long run back to the Broadway Pier. Off the starboard bow the harvest moon was rising huge and orange. We announced our closing song for the night; Gerry's excellent rendition of "Angel Baby". Everywhere I looked couples embraced and rocked slowly back and forth in a romantic last dance. When it ended, we were honored with loud applause from the appreciative audience.

The lady who hired us gushed with compliments as she counted out our pay for the night; two hundred dollars. The tip jar contained another hundred dollars. Three hundred dollars; sixty bucks each for having fun! We were all hooked on performing; that was a week's pay at minimum wage in four hours. I received a phone call the following day from the social lady; she had two more gigs for us.

Jim Conder was a talented vocalist who looked and sounded like Mick Jagger. He auditioned for lead singer and was hired on the spot. John Poppe was a sometimes-sulking James Dean type character who we brought aboard to play rhythm guitar. We had the perfect setup to cover Rolling Stones songs. It was eerie watching Jim perform; he was also an amateur actor and had perfectly mastered Jagger's facial expressions and movements. Our set list became heavy on Stones songs. Gerry continued with us for a while bringing down the house with "Heatwave" and other Motown covers.

We were working every weekend and the band was getting tight. After a performance at a local college I was approached by a young investor interested in a record deal; he would arrange and pay for studio time and reproduction costs. Once he had recouped his investment, we would split the earnings from record sales. He would also retain a professional song writer to pen two originals for our single forty-five record. We also agreed to this, which was a huge mistake. The songwriter was a washed-up Motown artist who came up with two original songs better suited to the Temptations than a Rolling Stones cover band. He hired two female backup singers and played the piano on one of the tunes; also, totally wrong.

The day finally came when we were ready to record our songs: "This Is the Day" and "Gypsy Heart". We crammed into my Plymouth Valiant station wagon and headed north to El Dorado Studios in Burbank. Television and music industry star Johnny Otis owned the El Dorado Studios and was present during the recording of our record. The recording was done on two tracks; one for instruments, the other for vocals. Most of the day was spent getting the instruments right. While the vocal track was being recorded Kenji and I sat in the soundproof observation room chatting with Johnny Otis; he had taken an interest in the group. Upon leaving he handed Kenji his business card and asked us to have our manager contact him, which he never did.

Getting airplay in major markets was difficult. We were not able to penetrate San Diego, but we got lots of time on air in the small outlying towns. "This Is the Day" made it into Escondido's top twenty. In El Centro we cracked the top ten. We got a lucrative gig offer from Pancho's, a teen nightclub in El Centro where we were becoming well-known. We got a taste of stardom at Pancho's. A mob of young admirers met us as soon as we pulled into the parking lot. We signed autographs for several minutes before going on with the setup. The windows facing out onto the street were frosted; the people on the sidewalk appeared as silhouettes. We were well into our first set when I saw numerous bobbing heads through the frosted glass. A crowd had gathered outside, and they were dancing. During our first break I went out the front door onto the sidewalk. I was met by a cheering group of fifty or so black youths. I signed more autographs and chatted for a while. I learned they were dancing on the sidewalk because they weren't allowed inside. That was the state of things in the 1960s.

The City of San Diego sponsored dances for the Baby Boomers at the Ocean Beach Recreation Center where the Inmates were regulars. The building was perfect; an expansive hardwood floor for dancing with a full-size elevated stage at one end. Here we could turn it up and shake the rafters. The place was always full of energy and packed for every performance. There would be at least one fight every night, usually started by one of the community's known pugilistic bad boys. The Masonic Temple on Sunset Cliffs Boulevard was another venue that hosted a regular schedule of dances. It too was always packed with OB and Point Loma locals. The dances were territorial; anyone from outside the area attended at their own risk.

After a good three-year run, the band days were coming to an end. It wouldn't be long before we all would be affected in one way or another by the war in Vietnam. We assembled for a party at Ma Kellogg's before our last performance. Ma's place had gotten the reputation as a party house to hooligans outside the neighborhood; music, chicks, and alcohol for all was the word on the street. It was only a matter of time before uninvited guests arrived on the scene. Most of the time the would-be party crashers were asked to leave and did so without incident, but not always.

On this occasion a gang of thugs showed up from across town wearing matching letterman club jackets, Sir Guy shirts buttoned all the way to the top, pointy boots, and khaki pants worn chest high. Their hair was slicked back and fastened in place by generous scoops of Pomade. The apparent leader was a big guy who wore a shiny Buck knife in a sheath on his belt. The gang entered the back yard from the alley; we went out to meet them. We faced off in a line and glowered at each other in silence.

The silence was broken when their leader made a crude suggestion to one of our girls. Someone threw a punch and the fight was on. What ensued was an outdoor barroom brawl, a melee; lots of swings, lots of misses, with an occasional blow landing. One of the blows landed on the point of the big guy's nose, which immediately began to bleed profusely. Enraged, he reached for his waistband and unsheathed his nine-inch Buck knife.

Everyone backed away quickly and froze. A commanding voice behind me ordered; "Put the knife down...put it down!" I looked around to see Ma holding a piece of 2x4 board and advancing. She stopped two feet short of the big guy and ordered again; "Drop the knife…Now!" He didn't drop the knife but grinned and spoke a vile insult having to do with Ma's haystack physique. Ma slammed the butt end of her 2x4 into his solar plexus doubling him over and causing the knife to drop to the ground. She wound up again and cracked him on the back of the head sending him to the ground.

The neighbors across the alley had called the police early on. Two squad cars pulled up in the alley seconds after Ma's knockout blow. The crashers were ordered to sit to await questioning while the cops sorted things out. The leader was still on the ground, semi-conscious. The nearby Buck knife was evidence enough that Ma had acted in self-defense. One by one the other crashers were interviewed. They were released when Ma refused to press charges. The cops ran a check on the leader; it revealed he was on probation for another crime. He was arrested and taken for medical treatment followed by booking in the downtown jail for assault and violating the terms of his probation.

And the party went on. It was a simple truth: To mess with Ma Kellogg was to open a can of bad Juju. Anyone who messed with Ma should not expect to escape unscathed.

7 BIG WEDNESDAY

Haggerty's

My family migrated west on Route 66 in 1952 with two other families. There was a boy my age in the caravan named Carl. His Aunt Bonnie and Uncle Mack had twin daughters and legal custody of Carl. Joan, Carl's mother and Bonnie's sister, was serving a prison sentence in Indiana for second degree murder.

Carl's father Mitch was a violent alcoholic wife beater. Mitch came home drunk and went berserk just before daybreak one Saturday morning. Carl, awakened by loud cursing, came into the dining room to find his mother pinned to the floor. His father was holding a phone aloft; he had just ripped it from the wall. He was going to crush Joan's skull.

Carl charged him and jumped on his back. Mitch turned on him in a rage. He grabbed Carl by the throat, punched him in the face, and flung him backwards into a china cabinet, breaking the glass doors and the cups and saucers within. The breaking glass and his wife's screams snapped Mitch out of his drunken rage. He grabbed his car keys and coat and stormed out of the house. Joan cleaned out Carl's wounds and arranged with sister Bonnie to watch over him for a few days. Joan went home, loaded a 12-guage shotgun with a single deer slug and waited for Mitch's return. A short while later the front door opened. Joan shot Mitch point blank in the face, blowing off the top of his head and killing him instantly.

Uncle Mack had a job waiting for him in California. He was hired by Wham-O Toys in Los Angeles to help develop the first Hula Hoop prototype. The toy became an international sensation making Wham-O millions of dollars. During the time Joan was incarcerated Mack prospered. He was able to buy a home in Palos Verdes with a spacious granny flat out back. Joan moved into the flat upon her release from prison and began spending time at Palos Verdes Cove. Joan was still young and attractive and got a lot of attention from the surfers who frequented the Cove. She met a guy her age that took a shine to Carl and offered to teach him to surf. They fell in love and were married the following year; Carl was officially adopted and had a real dad for the first time in his life. The family settled in Redondo Beach where father and son surfed together every chance they got.

Bonnie and my mother kept in touch by phone over the years. Mom would give me periodic updates on Joan and Carl's new life in Redondo Beach. One day the phone rang; it was Carl calling for me. He had heard through the grapevine that I was also heavily involved in surfing. Carl invited me up for an overnight visit and surf session at his favorite wave; a well-known spot called Haggerty's. It was October and the first winter swells were showing out of the north; ideal conditions for Haggerty's according to Carl. The following morning Kenji and I were on our way up the coast to Palos Verdes Estates; about 125 miles north of Ocean Beach. We were told to look for a church where we could park.

We found the church and pulled in at daybreak. The lot was already filling up with cars. I stepped out of the woody and was greeted immediately by Carl. He had grown a foot taller since we last saw each other. He was lean and tanned and looked like he just stepped out of a Surfer mag ad for Birdwell Beach Britches. I introduced him to Kenji, and he introduced both of us to his friend Kimo standing a few feet away. The days of uncrowded waves were long gone. The best spots were now guarded by territorial enforcers who could be vicious to outsiders. Being invited to the lineup by locals kept the angst to a minimum as long as you behaved yourself.

We descended the bluff and got a look at Haggerty's for the first time. It was a left-breaking point wave, a rarity in California. This morning the waves were perfect fun size; long lefts peeled into the cove one after the other; it was a Goofyfoot's paradise. Kenji had paddled into the lineup while Carl and I were reminiscing. We were still far from the takeoff zone when Kenji caught a head-high wave from the middle of the pack; a perfect peeling wall that morphed into a snappy shoulder. Carl and I stopped paddling briefly to watch the show and hoot aloud.

The next wave in the set was caught by Carl's friend Kimo. he was a stocky Hawaiian Goofyfoot with a beautiful red Jacobs 422 board; he had an aggressive style and was very good. We stopped again to watch the show and hoot some more. We traded waves for the next three hours. Completely surfed out, we all left the water at the same time. Back in the parking lot I invited Carl and Kimo to visit Sunset Cliffs where I could return the favor as a resident local. We declined Carl's offer to overnight and headed back to Ocean Beach with a stop at Captain Keno's in Leucadia to feast on double cheeseburgers and onion rings.

Carl Collins

In a couple of weeks, I was back on the phone with Carl. The first major northwest swell of the winter was lighting up Sunset Cliffs. I gave him directions to Ocean Beach, to Chris' Liquor, where I would meet him at seven the following morning. I drove to Luscombs Point that evening to do a final check. It was a brilliant winter evening; the setting sun dropped out of the clouds making for a spectacular sunset. A small pack of diehards was sharing perfect overhead waves in the gathering dusk. I drove to Ma Kellogg's to coordinate with Gale and Kenji. We decided to meet at Rockslide, a hard-breaking left that was usually less crowded than Luscombs.

I woke up before sunrise the following morning to the roar of breaking waves. During the big winter swells a salt mist hangs over the lower beach like a fog. I loaded up and headed for Chris' Liquor for coffee. The mist this morning was heavy requiring windshield wipers; the swell had come up overnight. I sat in front of Chris' waiting for Carl and growing concerned. I was never comfortable in heavy surf and today was going to be heavy. My latent fear of the water stemmed from a drowning in the family in 1933. My Mom's big brother, Jay Cook, drowned in the Ohio River at the age of fifteen; the only son in a family of four girls. Jay's drowning sent ripples through the next generation, as my Mother and aunts tried to keep me and my cousins away from water during our teen years out of fear that history might repeat itself. I felt I had an obligation not to drown; a heavy burden to carry.

Carl and Kimo pulled into Chris' parking lot right on time. They followed me to Rockslide where the others were already gathered. I got my first glimpse of the waves coming out of the early morning fog. The swell was huge and had overpowered the Rockslide reef. One continuous wall from below Rockslide all the way to Luscombs was closing out across the channels. We got back in the cars and drove the short distance to Ladera Street overlooking Garbage, a peaking wave that broke far offshore with deep channels on both sides. We watched several sets roll through in silence. It was big and ugly but holding in both directions.

Before the Leash

I introduced Carl and Kimo to Tinsley, Kellogg, and
Kenji's brother Gene. The aggressive Kimo had seen
enough; he pulled his red Jacobs 422 out of Carl's station
wagon and began waxing up. Kenji followed suit and
began preparations to lead the way down the perilous
cliff. The way down was a four-story vertical descent on
hand-carved footholds with a forty-pound longboard
under one arm and one free hand to balance with. At the
bottom was a shear ten-foot drop to the rocks that
required both hands. The board needed to be gently
lowered and stood upright at this point. The last ten feet
required finger and toe work. Once on the sandstone

ledge, you retrieved your board and started over the slippery rocks to the water.

I was one of the last ones down the cliff; today would test my limits. The waves looked huge from the top of the cliff and as everyone who surfed the Cliffs knew, it was always bigger than it looked from up there. I began the long paddle straight up the north channel between Garbage and a mushy right break called Intercourse, or North Garbage. The channel south of the main peak at Garbage was deep and rarely closed out. The north channel was not as deep, but still offered some refuge from set waves.

Gale Kellogg had never liked the long swims from the outer reefs. He had located an inside wave just north of the path down that he frequented. Here, the white water reformed over a deep hole into a swell that hit a shallow inside ledge creating a short snappy right. Gale always had the wave all to himself, and today was no exception. I waved to him as I passed by on my way outside. I reached the outside peak and took up a position on the shoulder; safely out of the impact zone. Carl was waving me over to the lineup; my caution was too obvious. I reluctantly started the paddle toward peak to join Carl and the others when someone yelled "Outside," and the scramble was on.

We all paddled furiously to sea for close to a minute before the first wave in the set rolled out of the mist into full view. It was an enormous black wall of water that stretched all the way from the south channel to Rockslide and beyond. We were paddling for our lives now. Everyone made it up and over the steep wall bringing the next wave into view. This one was bigger than the first and was feathering. The guys in the pit, out of breath and rubber-armed, knew they were screwed. Everyone but Gene Kozuma and Kimo pulled up short to let the wave break as far in front of them as possible before getting mowed down. Safe out on the shoulder I pulled up to watch Gene and Kimo scratching for their lives. For a second it looked like they were going to make it up and over the vertical face, but the feathering lip pitched over them midway up the face sucking them both backward "over the falls". The wave exploded over a huge boil; those who had pulled up short dove for the bottom; an instant later they were steamrolled by the wave, now a twelve-foot high wall of white water.

I was worried about Gene Kozuma. He was fearless, but not a proficient surfer; this day he was out of his depth from the beginning. I scanned the inside white water looking for swimmers. A group of three heads caught my eye; someone, Gene I presumed, was being tended to by two others.

I turned my attention back to the undulating horizon; another set, a bigger set, was coming. I was all alone now; the cleanup wave had taken everyone else. I pressed my face against the board and paddled hard for the horizon. I was soon in deep water and out of danger, floating up and over huge rollers and taking note for the first time of how far offshore I was. Looking north I could see Ocean Beach; to the south I could see the tip of Point Loma. It was only now that the danger was gone that fear set in. I was gripped by fear; my mind was running wild. If I succumbed to fear and panicked, I was going to drown. The swell was still building; how in the hell was I going to get back in?

My predicament brought to mind a terrifying surf story, one we all knew, that took place on Oahu in 1943. Two surfers, one a seasoned veteran the other a fearless teenager, took on big Sunset Beach on a rising swell. The swell built quickly, and soon the two were trapped outside. They paddled alongshore to Waimea Bay seeking a way in. The teenager, Dickie Cross, attempted a monstrous wave and was never seen again. Woody Brown, the seasoned vet, took a beating trying to come in and had to swim for his life. A group of servicemen likely saved his life; they spotted Brown, now semi-conscious, and pulled him from the shore break.

When the surf got this large the crowd in the water always shrunk to the same handful of brave souls; the rest of us became onlookers. Looking north, I spotted a pack of guys who had made it out to an offshore reef we called Indicator; they appeared as a half dozen specks north of Luscombs and way outside. I knew who they were from experience and could name them all even from this distance.

I got a grip on myself and looked at my options. There was only one; head for the beach come what may and hopefully pick off a makeable wave. I swung the board around and started for shore. I could see the path down the cliff at Garbage, so I had a good idea where the channel was.

After a few minutes of hard paddling I entered shallow water; the swells in the channel were feathering now and catchable. A little further inside a large wave crumbled gently directly in front of me. It was a wall of whitewater with some swell left at the bottom. I turned the board toward the beach and scooted back onto the tailblock; the instant before impact I dropped to the deck and hugged the board with all my strength. I came out in the clear on my belly right side up. I rose to my feet and rode the big mushy shoulder all the way inside, to where Gale was still on his inside spot. I paddled over and shared my war story, then caught a few fun reforms; my only real waves for the day. A short time later we both packed it in and headed back up the slippery path to the top of the bluff.

That afternoon we convened at Ma Kellogg's for a kegger; to celebrate being alive and swap stories from the day. Gene was there, alive and well, but still shaken from his experience. Kimo had been the first to realize Gene was in trouble; he too had gone over the falls and popped up near Gene in the whitewater. They were quickly joined by Carl and brother Kenji who held onto him until he regained his senses. Kimo's beautiful red Jacobs had been ripped away on impact and severely dinged on the rocks along with Gene's new Gordon & Smith. I put the crew on notice that they could count me out of any and all future big wave adventures. I was not a big wave rider; I had found my limit.

The evening turned to night and we all were getting a good buzz on. The girls showed up at dusk, prompting a re-telling of the big wave stories. Ma Kellogg set out a taco buffet on a backyard picnic table. It was a perfect ending to an unforgettable day. Carl and Kimo were far too toasted to make the drive back up the coast. Ma came out of the house with sleeping bags and pillows and set them up in the garage for the night. We stood for inspection one at a time when it was time to go; everyone passed Ma's DUI checkpoint except Tinman. As always, Mouse, the guy all our mothers wanted us to be, was there to save the day.

8 DECKHANDS

Days End; Cleaning the Catch

The creation of Mission Bay was in full swing in the late 1950s. The vast wetland known as False Bay was being dredged to allow boat navigation. The dredged sand was deposited in heaps to form islands surrounded by deep channels. The result would be a 4,000-acre public aquatic recreation area; the biggest in the country. Two new rock jetties that extended seaward several hundred yards were in place, and the channel between them was being dredged to a depth of twenty feet. Access to the open sea allowed the first deep sea fishing boats to begin operating out of Quivira Basin near the mouth of the bay. The kelp beds off Point Loma and La Jolla were teeming with life and were now just minutes away.

The first sport boat dock with shoreside support buildings was constructed in Quivira Basin in 1957. The Mission Belle, Spitfire, and La Jollan were among the first sportfishing boats to make regular runs out of Mission Bay. The period 1957-1959 were sensational years for fishing. The popular fish of the day was the Yellowtail, and they were everywhere. It was also a huge year for Bluefin Tuna and Albacore, but they were much further offshore, and most fishermen were not interested in the long boat ride to go after them. In the summer of 1959, a neighbor who I did lawn work for offered to take me out for Albacore; I jumped at the chance. The Spitfire was the long-range boat in the fleet. It was a painfully slow single diesel boat that seemed old even then. Somewhere on the other side of the Nine Mile Bank, with no fish in sight, the diesel sputtered and died. We drifted dead in the water for hours until the Coast Guard came to our rescue. We arrived back at the dock the next morning seasick, exhausted, and without a single fish.

My favorite boat was the La Jollan. I became a regular and was befriended by George Foster, the Captain. I was offered an after-school job prepping the boat for the next morning run. After a good day of fishing the boats returned with blood and scales coating the decks and rails. In summer months I filled in for the regular deck hands as needed. I got to fish when the action was slow and earned a free trip for every three trips worked. The half day boats in summer were packed with tourists who had no idea what they were doing. I got good at untangling "birds-nests," the term for hopelessly knotted up line.

F/V La Jollan

I continued to work the boats out of Mission Bay for several years. The main season ran roughly from May through September, the period of peak activity for both fish and tourists. The sportfishing fleet spent the winter tied to the dock; the migratory schools of game fish moved south out of range seeking warmer water. A handful of boats, including the La Jollan, ran daily winter trips for bottom fish; not very exciting to catch, but excellent eating. Bottom fishing was easy; a heavy sinker to speed your drop to the bottom with multiple hooks baited with squid or anchovies. On good days each drop produced four or five fish. Winching them up from the depths was more work than fun but when the reward was several delicious Red Snappers, it was well worth it.

I got a call from the Mission Bay Sportfishing office on a blustery January evening asking if I could work a bottom trip the next day. They also wanted to know if I could round up a second deckhand for the day. An earlier accident in the parking lot had resulted in both La Jollan deck hands sustaining injuries when they attempted to stop a loaded runaway dock cart. I recruited Trader Vic with a phone call and set out my gear for the morning. It was a nasty rainy morning when I picked up Trader for the trip. Driving across the San Diego River bridge we could see white caps as far as the eye could see. A small craft warning would probably be issued soon I was hoping, in which case the trip was off.

When we arrived at the dock, we were surprised to see around twenty hearty souls bundled against the weather and eager to fish. The skipper confirmed a small craft advisory was in effect, but the front was expected to pass; we were going fishing. We boarded the boat and began preparations to cast off. Most of the passengers were regulars; older retired friends who had fished the La

Jollan both summer and winter for years. I had fished with most of them before. They were knowledgeable and took care of themselves; and they were great tippers. We left the dock and headed for the bait barge anchored in the middle of Quivira Basin. There we loaded several scoops of live anchovies into the stern bait tank before heading to sea. With our work done for the moment, Trader and I lit cigarettes and went to the bow for the ride out of the channel. The passengers had taken shelter in the galley to escape the weather and drink coffee, leaving us alone on deck.

Getting in and out of Mission Bay in rugged weather was dicey. A sandbar was always building at the mouth creating a dangerous shoal that had to be dredged every several years. On this day the south side of the entrance was a treacherous swirl of whitewater. A deep spot on the north side was the only way out. The skipper held the boat slow and steady a hundred yards back waiting for a lull, then gunned it for the open sea. This is what we'd been waiting for: We took up positions standing on the bow deck. When the boat crested a steep wave, we both jumped into the air just before the boat dived down into the wave trough. The deck fell away leaving us suspended in mid-air for a couple of exhilarating seconds. We got in several good jumps before the boat cleared the jetties and angled north for La Jolla; it was time to get back to work.

Bottom fishing meant prepping frozen squid for bait to

supplement the live anchovies. Trader set about busting up the frozen five-pound blocks of squid and thawing them in the scuppers alongside the bait tank. I took my usual tour of the rack holding the outfits brought aboard by today's fishermen. Today's group was seasoned and well prepared; all the equipment was up to the task ahead except for two freshwater panfish poles that were woefully inadequate for sea fishing. I went to the rod locker and grabbed two outfits we kept for such occasions. When the owners came for their freshwater rods, I would pull them aside and hold school, then switch out their equipment.

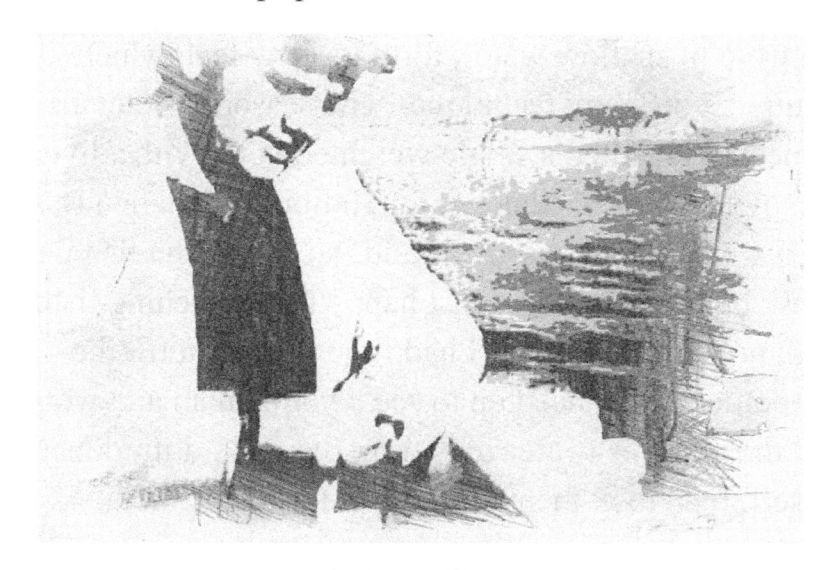

Trader Vic Prepping Squid

It was a rough ride to the fishing grounds; the boat pitched and rolled, taking continuous spray over the bow that kept the wheelhouse wipers going full speed. It was raining sideways again. The passengers were still holed up in the galley and getting seasick. I too was getting queasy, as was Trader. The skipper turned to starboard to enter La Jolla Cove which offered some relief from the pounding we were taking. We pulled into the Cove and dropped anchor in a spot protected from the southwest gusts by a towering headland and distant Mount Soledad. This was not ideal, but it was fishable until the weather improved. The sound of engines reversing and anchor chain clanging out brought the wobbly fishermen out of the galley. Several went directly to the rail and puked their breakfast into the sea. Others followed until a chum slick of vomit surrounded the stern.

We were in shallow water, forty to sixty feet, which required a different technique. The seasoned veterans immediately baited a single weighted hook with a live anchovy and dropped down for Halibut and Calico Bass. Soon we had hookups all around the boat. The fish were small, but everyone was just happy to be catching fish. With no gaffing needed, I had time to help outfit the newcomers. I glanced up to see a young man and woman pull the two freshwater rods from the rack. I introduced myself, then took them to the bow for a quick lesson.

The couple was young, about my age, and from the South. They introduced themselves as Johnny and Joyce; recently married and on their honeymoon. I fixed them up with rods from the boat locker and showed them how to rig their terminal tackle. I don't know if they heard a word I said; they never once took their eyes or their hands off each other as I rambled on. I showed them how to bait an anchovy, then went to the stern where an argument was taking place.

Trader was in the middle of it. A yard-long Halibut was banging around on the deck behind the bait tank. One of the old regulars was in a heated argument with a younger man over ownership of the prize Halibut. Trader pointed to the fish's head and chortled; "Take a look at this!"

There were two hooks firmly embedded in the Halibut's mouth. The fish had taken both baits just seconds apart, sending line screaming off both reels. The men fought alongside each other for several minutes unaware that they were fighting the same fish. Seconds before Trader gaffed it aboard it was obvious what had happened. I had seen this a few times before; rare but not unheard of. The solution offered in these cases was usually a coin flip, winner take all, or each fisherman takes half. In this case, they decided to share the fish and shook hands. Trader promptly filleted the Halibut and handed each man two beautiful thick fillets weighting several pounds.

After a couple of hours inside the cove, the bite slowed, the wind died down, and the rain stopped. The skipper ordered lines up on the PA, and we weighed anchor to head out to deeper water. There was a "secret spot" that everyone knew about a few miles off Windansea Beach. The water was several hundred feet deep; too deep to anchor. With the light breeze we could now drift fish.

When drift fishing the skipper positions the boat upwind and shuts down. Everyone congregates on the windward side and sends their heavy rigs as near the bottom as they can. Then it becomes a waiting game until the drift takes the baits over a reef teeming with fish. The rods quickly load up with Cow Cod, Snapper, Salmon Grouper, Barber's Poles, and a host of other brightly colored spiny bottom fish. Gaffs are rarely necessary. Instead we roam the deck with gloves and pliers unhooking and bagging fish and helping ladies and older folks winch the heavy loads up from the depths. It was our job to always be on the lookout for seals once fish started to come aboard. The skipper kept a 30-06 rifle in the wheelhouse to dispatch offending seals.

I went back to the bow to see how the young couple was making out. I found them both struggling with a heavy load of fish. I had put 5 hooks on each line and from the look of things, all 10 hooks had a fish on them. I took Johnny's outfit so he could help his wife who needed to be spelled. I saw color coming up below and yelled out for Trader. Johnny had a single fish, a huge Cow Cod. Trader gaffed it aboard; we stood back and marveled at the magnificent orange fish before turning our attention to the newlyweds. They had boated Joyce's fish and were celebrating with a giggly kiss; unfazed by the four colorful Snappers flopping at their ankles.

Scanning for Seals Aboard the La Jollan

We sacked the fish for the love birds and headed to the stern to wrap up. The skipper ordered lines up over the PA and the diesels roared to life; it was time to go home. Trader fetched the cleaning board and fixed it to the stern rail. I got out the scale to determine who won the day's jackpot. I ruled the filleted Halibut ineligible over the objections of the co-catchers and put three contenders on the cleaning board to be weighed. Johnny's Cow Cod handily beat out a Salmon Grouper and Ling Cod earning him the jackpot of sixty dollars.

I took the money to the bow where the newlyweds were still nibbling on each other. I handed Johnny the sixty bucks; a lot of money at that time. "Thank God, we needed this!" he said sincerely. I returned to the stern to find Trader Vic busy doing what Trader does;

entertaining passengers gathered around the bait tank by swallowing live anchovies, sticking them up his nose until nothing but their frantic tail fins showed, and challenging onlookers to do the same. There was always at least one taker in the audience who obliged.

The mouth of the entrance channel had calmed down a bit but was still treacherous on the shoal side against the south jetty. Once again, the skipper skillfully shot through the slot on the deep side of the channel, surfing a following sea into the calm waters of Mission Bay. Soon we were back at the dock tending the mooring lines and helping the fishermen disembark with their fishing gear and coolers. Trader fetched a cart into which we loaded the day's catch. This had been a good day; the cart was heavy. To make matters worse the tide was low, so the ramp was very steep. The loaded cart had gotten away from the regular deckhands yesterday which was why we had been called in. When all the fish had been loaded, Trader and I took positions behind the cart and got a running start that took us a third of the way up the ramp. After that it was a slow struggle to the top where the fishermen were waiting. Each gunny sack had a wire tag bearing a number issued to each fisherman at boarding. We called out the numbers until all the fish had been claimed; we were done for the day.

We were totally beat and starving with money in our pockets; it was off to the Midway Chuck Wagon where we could still get the lunch price; One dollar and seven cents for an all you can eat buffet. Trader Vic was no stranger to the Chuck Wagon management. It was rumored he held the record for number of trips through the buffet line at fourteen. The Chuck Wagon eventually went out of business, some say, because of Trader Vic and Nick Cordileone, another big eater and owner of the San Diego Bay bait barge.

What began as a joke by a local sportswriter got traction, culminating in the Golden West Classic Eating Contest, refereed by boxer Archie Moore and emceed by local broadcaster Regis Philbin. The contestants: Ernie "The Big Cat" Ladd, a three hundred pound plus football lineman for the San Diego Chargers, and local fishing community legend Nick Cordileone. The contestants consumed over forty pounds of food each, with Ladd winning by a mere three ounces of meat on a chicken bone that Nick overlooked.

I got a call late that evening asking if I could deckhand on the La Jollan for the rest of the week. One of the injured regulars had returned to work, the other guy quit. I agreed to fill in until a permanent replacement could be hired. The foul weather had blown through bringing smaller seas and lots of sunshine. The weather was fair, the tips were good, and my wallet was full by the end of the week. I was able to sleep in for the first time in several days.

I was awakened by a call from Kenji around nine in the

morning. He brought the news that a double murder had occurred the night before along the boardwalk in Ocean Beach. I got up and drove to the Newport parking lot. Cops were going door to door in the immediate neighborhood; the crime scene, out by the seawall at the base of the Silver Spray building, was sealed off. All the local news channels were in the parking lot, seeking interviews.

I drove up the hill to Ma Kellogg's. Kenji and Gale were in the kitchen listening to the radio news; the victims were a young married couple from out of the area with no known enemies. I left Kellogg's and picked up Mouse in the late afternoon. We drove up the coast to Del Mar to visit our pal Swabby Don who had recently relocated. The tragic day ended peacefully on Don's ocean-front deck with cold beer, burgers on the grill, and a spectacular ocean sunset.

The next morning, I picked up a San Diego Union paper and headed to Pete's for a Danish and coffee. I chatted with Pete and got situated at the counter. I opened the newspaper to find pictures of yesterday's murder victims; it was Johnny and Joyce, the young couple we had gotten to know on the La Jollan. I was dumbstruck; who in God's name would want to harm these people?

The Union Tribune article reported that the couple had gone for an evening walk on the boardwalk below the Silver Spray. They were shot to death by a sniper. The killer had fired five rounds from the top of the bluff, wounding them both. The killer slid down the pickleweed to finish them off with point blank shots to the head.

Bart Walters immediately came to mind. The night of the killings was moonless, and the tide was high; the hunting conditions Bart favored for killing seagulls. The initial shots came from a hiding place on the bluff, followed by point blank executions. The murder weapon was a .22 caliber rifle. I remember John telling me Bobby Price's chilling tale; that Bart finished off wounded seagulls at close range to silence their flapping and screeching. I could imagine the noise made by the wounded couple; praying aloud, calling out for help, reassuring each other. They had fallen at the base of the seawall; the killer slid down the pickleweed to get a direct line of sight for the shots that silenced them.

The murders rocked Ocean Beach; nothing like this had ever happened before. Speculation swirled among the residents as to who might have done the shooting. OB in 1964 was still a very isolated community. The consensus among my circle of friends was that the shooter was probably a local; one of us. Bobby Price was still living in Ocean Beach; surely, he would come forward to tell his story.

9 MEXICO

Hussong's Cantina Ensenada

Carl Collins and his parents were actively involved in humanitarian programs established by their Redondo Beach Christian Church. Two times a year, Christmas and Easter, they caravanned to Baja loaded with food, clothing, medical supplies, children's shoes and toys. One team stopped in the Tijuana River Valley slums. In addition to distributing supplies, skilled medical and dental congregants spent a week caring for the impoverished residents. A second team was bound for an

Ensenada orphanage. The third team continued further south to an orphanage near Santo Thomas.

I got a call from Carl two weeks before Christmas. He was driving the supply van going to Santo Thomas and invited me to ride along. I jumped at the chance; I had never been below La Bufadora at Punta Banda. There was room on top of the van for our boards and we were traveling alone. To me it was a golden opportunity to do something worthy and have some fun at the same time.

I met Carl at the Chris' Liquor parking lot just before Christmas. The van was actually a large walk-in truck like a plumber or milkman would drive. I strapped my board onto the roof, tossed the pillowcase with my belongings in the back, and we were off. Crossing the border in those days was a breeze. We crossed into Mexico around noon and reached K-38 a short time later. We got out to stretch our legs and check the surf. The lineup was empty and blown out. No matter, we had to be on our way. We were meeting the Ensenada team at the Baptist church where they would be working for the next week.

We turned off the paved road just past San Miguel and entered a colonia of humble dwellings. At the center of the colonia was the Baptist compound; a small neat church with several outbuildings. We found Carl's friends moving their things into one of the outbuildings, an old travel trailer, where they would spend the next week. The host church had prepared dinner for the Ensenada team; we were invited to join and gladly accepted. We entered the dining hall and got in line for the buffet of shredded beef tacos, salsa and frijoles. We took our plates to a card table where Carl's parents were saving two chairs for us. Gard Collins, Carl's stepdad, was a member of the pioneering Palos Verdes Cove crew. He and his friends had been featured in Surfer magazine articles; I was in the presence of a legend and a bit awe-struck. Joan, Carl's mom, rose to give her son a hug. She was a tanned, slender middle-aged lady who I knew so much about but had never met.

After introductions we took our seats; it wasn't long before the stories started. After listening spellbound to Gard recall the early days of Palos Verdes Cove, Joan had a request; a story she wanted Gard to hear. Joan had heard about the Cherry Cider Incident in Missouri when Carl and I were kids traveling west on Route 66 in a three-family caravan. Joan was serving time in prison for murdering her abusive husband and heard the story second-hand years later. We honored her request and told the story:

Our three-car caravan left Indiana on a hot August morning for the trip to California. I rode with my parents Betty Lou and Kenny. Carl was with his Aunt Bonnie and Uncle Mack in their beat-up Plymouth station wagon. Carl and I were six or seven years old at the time. Roy and Evelyn, a couple with a special-needs daughter, brought up the rear in their new Oldsmobile. We crossed the Mississippi River at St Louis and promptly got lost in the maze of city streets. When we finally found Route 66 West it was early afternoon; it was hot, and we were all parched. We saw the first of many Stuckey's billboards just outside of St Louis. Depicted on the large billboard was a jug of ice-cold cherry cider; thirty miles ahead. A half hour later the distinctive Stuckey's façade came into view. We pulled into the gravel parking lot and went inside to order. We came out with three gallons of frigid cherry cider, one for each family.

We sat at an outdoor picnic area and consumed every drop of the three gallons of cider. With our thirst quenched, we hit the road with Uncle Mack's beat up Plymouth in the lead. Looking back, it was amazing that not one of the adults knew about the laxative properties of cherry cider. It wasn't long after leaving Stuckey's that the first duet of high-pitched farts wafted in from the front seat. Fortunate for me, I was never fond of ciders and had opted for a soda instead. I found parents farting uncontrollably to be hilarious. The same scene was playing out in the other cars.

Up ahead was a Texaco sign. Mack turned into the gravel parking lot followed by Roy's Oldsmobile then us. The restrooms were twenty feet away. The car doors flew open; it was every man and woman for themselves. The men were gentlemen; they made a beeline for the dense woods behind the Texaco station. The three ladies were left to fight over the two toilets.

At this point, Joan asked her son a rhetorical question for Gard's sake: "And what about you son, what did you do?" "You know damn well what I did." He replied; "I dumped a load in my pants, opened a comic book and went on with life." Gard erupted in laughter mid-bite, showering us all with particles of food and knocking over his water glass.

We said our goodbyes and got back on the road to Santo Thomas. It was dusk now, and soon would be too dark to drive safely on the roads south of Ensenada. We breezed through a Mexican Army checkpoint and shortly thereafter came to the turnoff to Rancho Esperanza, our destination. The Rancho was a compound like the Ensenada Baptist's only much larger. It was home to a flock of orphans and the staff who cared for them.

Carl got out of the truck and was immediately mobbed by a cluster of kids calling his name. He had been coming down here for three years and had made lots of friends. Carl knew them all by name; he reached behind the driver's seat and pulled out a shopping bag full of goodies. He sat on the running board surrounded by his little admirers dispensing twinkies, mounds bars and potato chips until the bag was empty. When he went to the main building to report our arrival the kids tagged along behind like a gaggle of ducklings. It was a wonderful side of Carl that I was seeing for the first time.

The other members of the Santo Thomas team came to help unload the truck. We unrolled our sleeping bags on the floor of the cavernous cargo area and bedded down for the night. I was awakened in the morning by the ugliest dog I'd ever seen. It was standing over me licking my face and wagging its tail. Carl was already up and gone to join the rest of his team. The rear cargo door was ajar. I could see more curious animals sniffing and pecking outside. I slid out of the cargo door into a flock of chickens, the ugly dog right behind. Like it or not ugly dog would follow me everywhere I went for the next two days. I learned that the kids called him "Perro Feo". He was a smart and gentle beast, and I quickly took a liking to him. I briefly considered taking him back to the States, but I had no room for a pet of any kind.

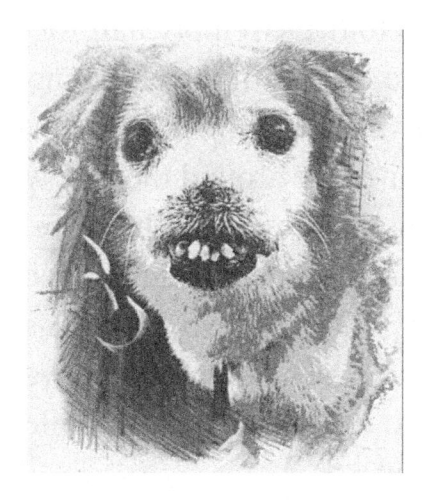

Perro Feo

That evening we gathered in the chapel for a special program put on by the children. The audience of volunteers and staff numbered around forty men and women. It was Christmas Eve; and an appropriately cold clear night for the celebration of the birth of Christ. The kids quietly took the stage in their choir smocks and mounted a small bleacher. Senora Ulloa, Rancho Esperanza teacher and choir director, waved her baton and the program began. The kids performed acapella versions of "Silent Night", "Away in a Manger", "Oh Holy Night", and "Oh Little Town of Bethlehem". Their harmonies were beautiful, nearly seamless; "Silent Night" gave me goosebumps and made my eyes water. The program concluded with the two oldest boys playing snare drums for the girl's performance of "Little Drummer Boy".

I awoke Christmas morning to Perro Feo licking my face; it was time to go to the assembly hall for the gift exchange. At the far end of the hall a mountain of wrapped gifts dwarfed a humble Christmas tree. The kids sat in a semi-circle around the tree while Senora Ulloa handed out the presents. She wore a red stocking cap, green elf's apron, and plastic reindeer horns for the occasion. Every child got two fun gifts sent down by Carl's congregation. The grand finale was the handing out of new shoes; the only shoes the children would have for the year ahead.

Drawing a child's name from a hat was an annual event

usually conducted around Thanksgiving. Participating church members were each assigned a child and provided with their shoe size and preferences. A week before the trip to Mexico a wrapping party potluck was held in the church fellowship hall and the wrapped boxes distributed to the teams. I was deeply moved by these children who had nothing, yet were typical giggly kids; happy kids, thanks to the love shown them by an amazing group of people I was fortunate to know.

We were awakened early the following morning by the roar of a descending helicopter. Clouds of dust settled on the compound; small stones and debris stirred up by the propwash pinged against the side of the truck. I had noticed the day before that the hill behind the compound had been graded off for no apparent reason. I exited the truck and looked to the top of the hill; the graded area was a helipad; the noisy helicopter had just touched down and was idling. The chopper was painted a striking bright June Bug green, and emblazoned with the letters "SAFA"; apparently a company name. Three men exited the copter; two wore business suits and the third carried a roll of blueprints. The blueprint man was pointing seaward, as if giving a presentation to the men in suits. After ten minutes or so the men got back in the chopper, the engine revved, and the compound was once again showered with clouds of dust and stinging pebbles as it lifted off.

I turned to Carl; "What the hell was that?" "Developers"

he answered. "There's a plan to turn this entire area, seven hundred acres, into a high-end resort with a golf course, high-rise waterfront hotel, and restaurants." "What will happen to Rancho Esperanza and the kids?" I asked. "We don't know" he replied. We said our goodbyes and headed down the bumpy dirt road to the highway. Ugly Dog trotted along behind us until we reached the paved road. I exited the truck and gave him one last poignant hug and chin scratch; he cried and pleaded with me with huge sad eyes. It worked; I opened the cargo door and he jumped in. I had a dog now.

We got into Ensenada that afternoon. With our mission complete, it was time for a cold beer at Hussong's Cantina. It was not unusual to find neighbors from OB in Hussong's; a trip to Ensenada always included a stop at the Cantina. Everyone had a Hussong's story. We finished our beer and hit the road for home. Just outside of Tijuana we picked up two hitchhiking hippie types. We were just several hundred feet from the border when the hitchhikers informed us, they were holding drugs; four rolls of Benzedrine to be exact. Carl ordered them out of the truck; they would have to walk across. It was early evening and we hadn't eaten since we left Rancho Esperanza. Carl agreed to wait at the San Ysidro Jack in the Box until the they caught up with us, then take them as far as San Diego. We crossed the border and pulled into the San Ysidro Jack in the Box. We took our cheeseburgers and fries to an outdoor table and waited. I bought two burgers for the dog and fashioned a water bowl out of a paper cup so he could have a drink. I was munching on my cheeseburger pondering a name for my new dog when a billboard across the street caught my eye. It was an advertisement for Jim Beam. That's it, I thought; it was meant to be. "Perro Feo" was now "Whiskey!"

The hippies didn't show up; nearly an hour had gone by and we were ready to move on when the duo finally appeared. They jumped into the cargo bay; they looked pale and shaken. They had been pulled aside for a secondary inspection. They had hidden the tinfoil-wrapped rolls of Benzedrine between their cheek and gum. As the inspector was preparing to shine a flashlight in their mouths, they swallowed the rolls; twenty bennies each, and were now clutching their chests expecting their hearts to explode. Carl offered to take them to the nearest hospital Emergency Room in Chula Vista, just a few minutes north. They declined, fearing arrest on drug charges more than a possible heart attack.

I was in favor of leaving them there if they didn't want medical attention. I could see the clear possibility of being arrested as an accessory to attempted drug smuggling. Carl had another idea; he had completed EMT training and knew what to try next. We drove into San Ysidro a short distance and pulled into a supermarket parking lot. Carl was back five minutes later with Ipecac syrup and two bottles of warm clam juice. He ordered the frightened hippies to split the bottle of Ipecac and wash it down with a pint of the warm clam juice; they eagerly complied. Back on Highway 101 North, it didn't take long before both victims were puking their guts up.

We dropped the pair off in Old Town to continue their trip home. They were feeling much better, euphoric in fact. The bennies had kicked in full force and they were chattering like Magpies. They thanked us profusely before sticking out their thumbs to solicit another ride. The euphoria wouldn't last; it would be three days before they slept again. By that time, they would be grinding their teeth to powder and scratching their itchy skin until it bled.

10 CHURCH ROW

Ocean Beach First Baptist Church

My mother, Betty Lou, drew her tremendous strength from her unshakable faith in Jesus Christ. She had come from rural Indiana where her family had farmed for generations. She was left on her own when my twin siblings were six months old. Sunday was church day for the entire family: In the morning there was a worship service followed by Sunday School. In the evening we attended a second worship service. Wednesdays were prayer meeting nights, followed by a meeting of the young adults group known as the Builders. I faithfully attended Sunday services, but only because Mom insisted on it. I spent my time in the pew daydreaming and doodling on offering envelopes. The primary allure of Sunday School was the two-dozen or so cute girls that attended regularly.

OB's "Church Row" was on Sunset Cliffs Boulevard between Brighton and Santa Monica. In the sixties everyone went to church. Our family belonged to the First Baptist congregation. The Methodist Church was right across the street. The impressive Sacred Heart Catholic Church took up half of the next block. Many of my childhood friends attended nearby Sacred Heart School. The Lutheran church was on the corner of Cape May, and the Episcopal church on the corner of Brighton. Church Row was bustling with activity every Sunday morning; attendance was at an all-time high for all denominations.

My trip to Mexico with Carl was an eye-opening experience. I was touched by the smiling kids who had nothing materially but were rich spiritually; they had mastered gratitude. The kids were grateful for what little they had, and generously shared what they had with others. I started taking a greater interest in Christianity in general, and the Baptist missions to Tijuana in particular.

We had a sister church at the west end of Tijuana, above the river valley slums. From the front porch of the humble adobe church I could see Point Loma clearly; the expansive bay view homes of La Playa glistened in the distance, clusters of boats with billowing white sails from the San Diego Yacht Club competed in the blue waters off Coronado Roads. Lowering my gaze to the Tijuana River Valley I observed a sea of shanties constructed of cardboard, sheets of rusted corrugated metal, old tires, tarps, and miscellaneous pieces of junk. Our hosts took us inside for a noon meal of wilted lettuce and tomato salad, tortillas, and warm Kool Aid. Trader Vic had arrived at his own spiritual crossroads at the same time; he started attending OB Baptist Church along with the family. Mouse and Tinman joined us from time to time as did the girlfriends. Both Trader and I took the message to heart and were baptized into the church on the same Sunday night a few months later.

I drew closer to my Mother as my own faith grew. Our relationship had often been contentious. Mom felt the stress of providing for four kids; I was burdened with heavy responsibility that I sometimes didn't handle well. Both of us said things we later regretted, but at the end of the day we were good. My woody was our family car and I was the only driver. Mom had never driven a car and was not comfortable with the thought of driving on San Diego's busy highways. I convinced her it was time to learn how to drive. The stick-shift woody turned out to be too much of a challenge. She had some money saved up, so we went looking for a car with an automatic transmission on the used car lots along El Cajon Boulevard.

Women had it tough in those days. Every so often Mom would come home from work in tears because a new man she had trained six months ago was now her boss. A divorced woman was stigmatized as some other man's problem; something less than. And it wasn't just the men who could be cruel; happily married women could be even more vicious and condescending, figuring a divorcee must be loose and a temptation to their husbands.

So, I wasn't surprised when we went car shopping that the salesmen would push the crappiest car on the lot, the one no one else would buy. It was after dark and we had worked our way along the Mile of Cars to East San Diego. We walked onto a brightly lit lot with pennants and balloons flying. We were greeted by a tall skinny middle-age man who peeled back his lips and whinnied like a horse when he laughed. He was a funny guy who bore an uncanny resemblance to Mom's favorite brother-in-law. Somewhat smitten, she asked for his recommendation and, of course, he had one.

He shouted out orders to the lot attendants to retrieve a car from the rear of the lot. Soon, the attendant drove up in an immaculate 1963 Chevy Corvair station wagon. I had skimmed a recent book by Ralph Nader that made the Corvair out to be a death trap. I tried to pull Mom aside, but she was sold; the car was more than she wanted to spend but it was in beautiful condition. The salesman whinnied his delight and disappeared into the office with my driver's license. Once we were alone, I told Mom all I had read about the Corvair. She was sold; we were going on a test drive, but she did agree to pray over it more to satisfy me than anything. We held hands, closed our eyes and she said a brief prayer; "Lord Jesus guide us we pray, if it is not thy will that we buy this car please send us a sign, Amen."

I took my place behind the wheel and turned the key. It sounded kind of like a VW bug, and, like the VW the engine was in the rear. We pulled out onto El Cajon Boulevard and headed east. Mom rode shotgun; the salesman sat in the rear seat with sister Donna. My twin brothers kneeled in the rear cargo area, making faces at the cars behind us. We passed a Chicken Delight delivery truck with an enormous fiberglass chicken riding in the bed. I made a lame joke, something like; "Look out for Chicken Delight trucks, the drivers are always in a *fowl* mood!" From the back seat came an overdone patronizing whinny that went on for ten seconds.

The Corvair was fun to drive; I found myself hoping we could do the deal. It was low on power and loud in the cabin when accelerating but it handled much better than expected, and it had an automatic transmission. I made a loop onto University Avenue and headed back to the car lot. We were all in a festive mood; Mom was excited about her first car, the salesman was delighted, and all was going well. I turned off University and headed up a side street to the car lot. That's when I first smelled something out of the ordinary; something was wrong. It grew quickly from a faint odor to the overpowering stench of burning wire insulation. We were approaching the car lot with a line of cars behind us. As we approached the stop sign at El Cajon Boulevard, the engine burst into flames. I pulled the Corvair off the road and onto the sidewalk at the base of a stop sign.

The salesman leaped out of the car and started beating the flames with his coat. I pulled my brothers from the back of the car and we all moved away a safe distance.

The engine fire ignited the stop sign, which in turn set the fluttering car lot pennants ablaze. Salesmen and lot attendants came running with fire extinguishers, but it was too late; the Corvair was engulfed in flames. Now they turned their attention to saving the other cars on the lot. Flaming plastic pennants were raining down on the cars, igniting the cardboard price signs on the windshields. We heard distant sirens converging from both directions. We walked back to the side street where the woody was parked. Mom and I agreed without speaking; her prayer for a sign had been answered. I pulled onto El Cajon Boulevard and drove by the car lot. Two fire engines were on the scene dealing with the Corvair. Two lot employees were on the roof of the dealership snuffing out spot fires with a garden hose.

Our adventure made for good story telling at church the following Sunday and led to discussions of "Signs from Heaven" in general. I couldn't rationalize God torching a Chevy Corvair and nearly burning down a car lot when something less involved would have done the trick. If the car had refused to start for instance; I would've been fine with that.

The OB Baptist men had a softball team; I was invited to play. The Phillips men were above average baseball players going way back. I had played Little League and Pony League ball in the OB leagues and done well. This would be my first experience playing softball. It was a far easier game than hardball. The pitches came in slow, belt high, over the plate, and easy to crush. The skill level on our church team ranged from good to awful. Joey Ahern, the team captain, was a good ballplayer as were his two ringer friends he had brought aboard. I carried the highest average on the team and batted either third or cleanup in the order. At the other end of the spectrum was Steve Hines. His team nickname was "Barney" due to his uncanny resemblance to Don Knotts, Andy Griffith's Mayberry deputy. In fact, most of his teammates didn't know his real name was Steve. Half the men on the team had never played in an organized league; they were there for the Christian fellowship. Barney had never picked up a bat or glove. He didn't know the basic rules of the game which resulted in some hilarious moments.

It was in the middle innings of our fourth league game before Barney reached base for the first time. We were playing the team from College Avenue Baptist; a decent team just behind us in the standings. Barney hit a dribbler down the third base line that died in the grass making a tough play for the third baseman. The throw to first was wide, pulling the first baseman off the bag. Barney raced past the bag missing it entirely. It was a live ball and he could be tagged out. When the first baseman came to apply the tag, Barney made no effort to get back to the bag; instead he took off running into right field with the first baseman in hot pursuit. The pair ran past the bewildered outfielders then angled back toward the diamond. Barney arrived back on first base ahead of his pursuer and bent over to catch his breath. When he looked up, he was perplexed by the laughter coming from both dugouts. To his dismay, the umpire had regained his composure and made the call; "You're Out!"

Our first baseman's name was Frank. He was an above average player but only had one leg; the other had been amputated at the knee. He wore a prosthetic device although you'd never know it. He ran with a limp and was slow of course, but no one knew he had an artificial leg; not even some of the guys on the OB Baptist team. Frank was a good place hitter. He specialized in opposite field line drives to right. We were playing a night game against the Methodist team when things went wrong. Frank hit a Texas League pop up to right field behind the first baseman. The pitcher rushed to cover the vacated bag. He was looking at the first baseman, anticipating the toss and ran into Frank who was also running at top speed. Both Frank and the Methodist pitcher went flying. The dust settled revealing a ghastly sight: Frank's artificial leg had broken free, leaving an empty space in his trouser leg between his stump and the top of the prosthesis. Everyone thought his leg had been knocked from its socket and horribly fractured. Everyone rushed to the scene; a Methodist player ran to the recreation center to call for an ambulance. Those of us in the know formed a circle around a mortified Frank while he re-attached his leg. The game went on. Two hours later at our after-game place everyone including Frank was recalling the horrified look on the Methodist pitcher's face and howling with laughter.

We ended the season tied for first place with our nemesis, Christ Lutheran. The team was led by the church's pastor, an intense guy who believed in winning at any cost. He had his team on the field doing calisthenics a full hour before game time. Exercise hour was followed by a center field team prayer to petition God's support in the upcoming contest. The pastor had recruited some impressive ringers from the surrounding neighborhood; less than half of his roster were actual members of the Christ Lutheran congregation, and most of them were consigned to the bench during playoffs. The pastor expected perfection; players making defensive errors could expect to be loudly chewed out in front of their teammates. I noticed during warmups that one guy in particular, an obvious ringer wearing the number 13, was fed up with the pastor's tirades. After mis-playing a grounder during infield practice he was barked at. As soon as the pastor looked away number 13 threw his glove to the ground and thrust both middle fingers high in the air for all to see.

It was a good game. Both teams played error free ball through six innings; the lead had changed four times. We came to the last inning tied 6 to 6. Christ Lutheran failed to score in the top half. We were Home Team and could win the game now with a single run. We were batting the bottom of the order; the first two batters grounded out, bringing up Barney who batted last in the lineup. I grabbed my glove and prepared to take the field for extra innings. To everyone's surprise, Barney laced the first pitch into shallow left field for a clean single. The left fielder, number 13, charged the ball and snagged it on the first hop. He fired a rocket to first base ahead of Barney; the throw went high to the right, allowing Barney to take second base. The pastor was livid. Now we had the top of the order coming up. Joey crushed the first pitch into left center for what appeared to be a clean double. Barney was now scrambling for third base. I was the third base coach; I gave him the green light to go for home.

Just as Barney rounded the bag, Number 13 got to the ball, set himself, and fired a canon shot to home plate. This time his throw was on target. I heard the pop of the ball hitting the catcher's glove when Barney was still three feet away from home. The catcher turned to apply the tag; Barney slid the last three feet and appeared to get a foot across the plate before the tag; the call could go either way. The umpire paused for moment, then emphatically gave the "Safe" sign. The team poured out of the dugout for a celebration at home plate. We lifted Barney onto our shoulders and carried him off the field. He was the hero; it was a moment he would never forget. The league president and his wife were next to the bleachers where they had set up a card table full of trophies. There was a brief ceremony to hand out the small individual trophies. The team captain accepted the impressive team trophy which would be displayed in the OB Baptist fellowship hall. Barney was voted game MVP and was awarded the game ball which all of us had signed.

Our celebration was interrupted by loud swearing coming from the dirt infield. Number 13 was faced off with the Christ Lutheran pastor on the pitcher's mound. The outfielder was being berated by the livid pastor for his errant throw that put Barney on second base and set up the winning run; "You cost us the championship! You had one thing to do and you blew it; you screwed up!" Number 13 had had enough; "Shove it up your righteous ass! I quit!" Number 13 turned to walk away; the pastor tackled him from behind and they fell to the ground. The pair rolled around in the dirt between the pitcher's mound and second base, trading blows to the head with closed fists. That's how we left them; punching it out in the dirt. Their Christ Lutheran teammates knew what was coming and had left before us.

11 THE LAST LUAU

Carl's Greeting from the President

The Vietnam draft would soon rock our world and scatter us to the far corners of the globe. Trader Vic, Mouse, Tinman, and Swabby Don were already gone. Kenji and Gale had received their draft notices to report for active duty, effectively putting an end to the Inmates. Up north, Carl Collins and his buddy Kimo Kahale had also received their orders to report for induction. The rest of us were on the bubble. I still had a hardship deferment but would soon lose it.

We decided to throw one last party; a farewell party, a grand luau. A planning meeting was held in Ma's kitchen for an epic bash to be held on the following Saturday. Kenji and I volunteered to do a same-day dive for fish and abalone and bring them to the party skillet-ready. Tom was put in charge of entertainment; he worked in the audio-visual department at San Diego State College and had access to first-run movies. The girls would provide decorations and side dishes; the guys would groom the backyard and set up tables and chairs.

I picked up Kenji and headed for Sunset Cliffs the morning of the party. The surf was small and the water clear; a good day to dive. We brought a burlap bag hung from an inner tube to hold our catch. We always drew straws to see who towed the inner tube back from the edge of the kelp beds a half-mile from the beach. Towing a bag of bleeding fish to shore sometimes attracted uninvited guests.

Kenji was a good free diver, and my usual dive partner. Our favorite destination was a ledge at the inner edge of the kelp forest directly off Pescadero Beach. The ledge might have been a shoreline from an earlier time. It ran parallel to the coast in twenty-five feet of water. Under the ledge the abalone were stacked one on top of the other. On good days we quickly got our limit and turned our attention to spearing fish. We took up positions several yards apart in the floating kelp and sat motionless making as little noise as possible. Through the water column below us swam fish going this way and that. It usually didn't take long before a good fish came into view. We both carried kelp guns; rubber powered spearguns shortened for use in the close confines of the kelp forest.

By noon we had ten nice abs in the bag. A quick-moving school of Yellowtail breezed through while we were working the ledges for abs. Kenji managed to spear one that appeared to be around ten pounds. We just needed a few more fish and we were done for the day. The Calico Bass were everywhere that day. I speared a nice one, four pounds or so, and tossed it in the game bag. Kenji followed with another Calico about the same size. I went down again for one more good fish. I had found a big patch of sandy bottom next to the ledge; I sensed there was a halibut there hunkered down hiding in the sand.

Kenji Kozuma

I was in twenty feet of water holding on to the top of the ledge scanning the sand patch for the outline of a halibut when the biggest round stingray I had ever seen came out of the dark right toward my face. Startled, I drew my gun up and shot from the hip scoring a direct hit. That was a big mistake; I should have just moved out of the way and let the ray swim by. I went to the surface to remove the ray from my spear. I made my second mistake; I let the fish slide down the shaft and land atop my left hand. In an instant the ray buried his stinger in the palm of my hand, nearly going all the way through. When the stinger came out blood shot out of the wound and an instant searing pain started moving up my wrist. I dropped the gun and called out to Kenji that I had to get to shore. I left him with the bag and started swimming toward the beach which seemed a million miles away. With every heartbeat the searing pain moved a little further up my arm. When it reached my elbow, I started to panic. I had heard that upper body stings could kill you; now the pain was in my shoulder headed toward my heart.

A guy in the lineup at Pescadero somehow sensed I was in trouble and came out to meet me. He slid off his board and shoved it to me. Now I was making good time; the panic subsided, and I started planning my moves once I reached the beach. I caught a wave and bellied it out; it delivered me to the sand. I charged up the path to my car and drove several blocks to Dr. Greaves' office on Cable

Street. I was sent to the front of the line and taken to an examination room. I was immediately given a shot of Demerol. Within seconds the agony became a pleasant throb from my shoulder to my swollen hand. Dr. Greaves showed up a few minutes later and gave me a tetanus shot before thoroughly cleaning the gaping wound in the palm of my hand.

Kenji was waiting for me when I came out of the examination room. He had tossed the gun with ray still attached into the gunny sack and towed the inner tube back to the beach. He left our gear in the keeping of the Good Samaritan and set out on foot for the doctor's office. I was thankful Kenji came to get me; I was high on narcotics and in no shape to drive. With Kenji behind the wheel we returned to the beach to get the gear and thank the guy who gave up his board. My gratitude quickly turned to anger upon discovering the Good Samaritan had left, taking our game bag with him; ten fat Abalone, five Calico Bass, and a Yellowtail.

It was getting close to party time. I was wounded and spaced out on Demerol; Kenji was exhausted. Only one thing to do; go to Point Loma Seafoods. It was an embarrassment for skilled hunters like us to have to buy seafood from a market. We vowed to keep it just between us. We pooled our money and came up with enough to buy a half-dozen cleaned Abalone and ten pounds of fresh Rock Cod. We left Point Loma Seafoods penniless. At least the fish were filleted, and the abs pounded and sliced. It was time to get cleaned up head for the party. The Demerol had worn off and the pain in my hand had returned, but I was good to drive again. I dropped Kenji off at his house to ice the seafood. I went home, showered, and donned my luau outfit. I drove to Ma's using my good hand to steer, parked on the street and entered the backyard from the alley; it was a sight to behold:

Tom had scored a first run movie; *Cool Hand Luke*, staring Paul Newman. A bedsheet hung neatly over a concrete block wall served as the screen. Folding chairs were arranged theatre style with an aisle; a formidable looking sixteen-millimeter projector from San Diego State's AV Department rested on a rolling cart behind the seats. The girls had transformed the scruffy backyard into an outdoor ballroom. They strung lights and crepe paper aloft from the roof of the house to the garage on the alley. Fairy lights in the shrubbery added an elegant touch. Gale and the boys fashioned a fire pit from concrete blocks and lit it off. They placed several folding tables end to end to form one long communal table and covered it with linen tablecloths held in place by polished abalone shells.

Kenji and I set up the ab skillet over the fire pit to heat up. Our ab skillet was a jumbo wok two feet in diameter with a long wooden handle to work it with. Carl and Kimo arrived next with their girlfriends. They brought an unexpected treat; several pounds of clams dug that morning in Redondo Beach. Ma set up a buffet table for the side dishes that would be arriving soon. Gale set up a turntable on a TV tray just outside the door to his room and put on an LP of classic 1940's Hawaiian music. The girls showed up at dusk bearing side dishes and looking lovely in their colorful sarongs, flower leis and sandals.

We tapped the keg of Pabst Blue Ribbon and I set about introducing our friends from Redondo Beach to other members of the tribe. After mingling long enough to get a good buzz going, we sat down at the communal table for the feast. Carl said grace, imploring the Lord to keep us all safe from harm in the uncertain days to come. Carl was handsome and debonair, a fact that did not go unnoticed by the ladies in attendance. Carl was also a solid guy who lived an exemplary Christian life; he walked the walk. I gave him huge credit for not succumbing to bitterness and depression after enduring his nightmarish, violent childhood.

Four turkey platters of steaming seafood were arranged in a line down the middle of the table. One platter contained Abalone steaks, fresh rolls and tartar sauce. There were two platters of seared Rock Cod fillets garnished with cilantro and sundried tomatoes. The last platter was piled high with steamed clams in the shell. A quart crock of melted butter was positioned at each end of the table, along with two bowls of lemon wedges. On the side we had to-die-for mac and cheese and a potluck standard, green bean casserole. For dessert, there was homemade vanilla ice cream and blueberry cobbler. I quickly satisfied my hunger and went into sport eating mode, trying at least one helping of everything on the table. We were all stuffed and unbuttoned by movie time. One by one we waddled to our theatre seats to watch *Cool Hand Luke*.

Set in the late '40s we see ne'er do well Luke (Paul Newman) using a pipe cutter to chop off the heads of parking meters, too drunk to be worried about the cops who arrive on the scene to arrest him. Luke ends up on a road crew chain gang working in blistering heat supervised by a sadistic overseer. The chain gang scenes were super realistic, from the grasshoppers chirping in the background to the beads of sweat on the inmates' care-worn faces. Time and time again Luke escapes only to be recaptured and beaten. The best scene in the movie was Luke's confrontation with the sadistic Captain of Road Prison 36: Luke is returned to the road gang after yet another failed escape attempt and placed in manacles. The Captain beats Luke to the ground in front of the other inmates and proclaims; "What we have here is a failure to communicate". Luke emerges as an unbreakable hero, standing up to "The Man" with wit and that easy smile.

We gathered around the fire pit after the movie and broke out the ukuleles. Kimo, a transplant from Oahu, led the song circle with some traditional Hawaiian tunes; everyone fell silent, awed by Kimo's skilled playing and rich baritone voice. I studied the faces of my friends in the circle, lit by the flickering fire. I was suddenly overcome with melancholy; we would be going our separate ways soon and would not see each other again for a long time. And there was the eventuality no one wanted to talk about; that one or more of us would never return.

It was two in the morning and finally time to say our goodbyes. Carl, Kimo and their dates made the rounds hugging everyone before heading back to Redondo Beach. I gave Carl a parting hug and admonished him to take good care and write often. We all pitched in and cleaned up Ma's yard, put away the tables and chairs, and washed the dishes. We returned to the dying embers in the fire pit and sat together one last time. It was near dawn and quiet; only the soft roar of the distant surf could be heard. The luau was a milestone; it marked the end of a chapter in our lives, a great chapter. Life in OB would never be the same again.

12 LOBSTERMAN

F/V Flora Wynn

The late '60s were financially hard for my family. While Mom's earnings remained relatively stationary, the cost of supporting a family of four had gone through the roof. I applied for, and was granted, a hardship deferment from the draft. I located a financial backer and started a lobster fishing business. I bought an old wooden lobster skiff on a rusted-out trailer and spent the weeks leading up to the season making her pretty and seaworthy. I named the skiff after my great-grandmother, Flora Wynn. I was only two years old when Grandma Wynn passed. The story told to me later in life was that Flora's final request was to be buried holding a bouquet of flowers picked by me and bearing my name; her request was honored.

The F/V *Flora Wynn* was a basic lobster boat, twenty feet

long, and powered by a 1958 Johnson outboard motor. Most of us had tiller-steer setups with pipe tiller extenders allowing us to stand and steer from the middle of the boat. For balance, we ran a taut line from the point of the bow to hold onto with our free hand. I had a good compass for foggy mornings, but no radio and no lifejacket which was normal for that time. I ran fifty traps out of Islandia Marina in Quivira Basin. My assigned fishing sector started at the Mission Bay entrance jetty and ran south to Cal Western College; familiar territory.

I soon discovered lobster fishing was backbreaking work. I made my own traps. I bought several rolls of wire mesh and fabricated my cages in the front yard of our Pescadero duplex. Ballast bricks were inserted into the traps to help keep them stable on the bottom. Each trap had two chicken wire funnels and a hinged door on top. A cylinder of chicken wire stapled to the middle of the trap held the bait. Each trap required at least sixty feet of heavy line, and a wooden buoy bearing my Fish & Game number; L225D. During the week preceding the season opener we dropped our traps. The day before the season opener we were allowed to bait them.

Lobster season normally starts off with a bang. For the first few weeks every trap comes up loaded with lobster. We all carried a metal measuring device that looked like a pocket comb with no teeth. You placed one end between the lobster's eyes, and the other at the rear of the carapace. If the comb was longer than the carapace, the lobster was short and had to be tossed back. For every legal bug I took, I threw back a half-dozen shorts. Most of the shorts were what we called "hair liners"; only a sixteenth of an inch or so undersized. When the fishing got slow later in the season it became increasingly hard to throw back the shorts. Most of us came up with ways to keep the hair-liners without getting caught. I designed and built a trap twice the size of the others. It had no bait cage or funnels; just a large hinged door on top. I dropped it about a quarter mile off Pescadero; I named it "Big Bertha".

In my sector the game wardens kept an eye on us with powerful scopes from their cars parked in the turnouts along Sunset Cliffs. The warden that worked the Cliffs most days was a heavy-set man we called "Inks"; you had to assume he was always watching. When the catch began to dwindle, I began dropping the hair liners to the bottom of the boat with my back turned to the shore, then I would theatrically toss a stone to make a convincing splash of the short being released.

At the end of the day I pulled Big Bertha and deposited the shorts I had collected. Later under cover of darkness me and my accomplice paddled our longboards out to Big Betha and collected the booty. This worked out great until the foul weather arrived in late December. I devised another scheme: The shorts were placed in a gunny sack and hung over the boat transom. Twenty feet or so of light rope was tied to the gunny sack; at the other end of the line I tied a small fishing bobber. My business partner's son was my accomplice. I would hug the jetty coming in, and discreetly drop the bag at the jetty boulder he had splashed with white paint. My partner then came out of hiding and cast a snag-hook to pick up the line and retrieve the bag full of lobster.

I quickly learned that the prospect of free lobster brought out the criminal in otherwise law-abiding citizens. Just a short distance offshore there was no law: it was the Wild West. Surfers in pairs raided our traps in the middle of the night from shore. Clueless weekend boaters would stumble across our buoys and pull them up, then gleefully steal all the lobsters therein. For night raiders we devised a deterrent; three feet of hatpins skewered through the trap rope ten feet below the surface. It didn't stop the poachers, but it slowed them down. On calm weekends when recreational boaters took to sea, some of us took to anchoring up in the middle of our field of traps to stand guard.

Late in my last fishing season the going got rough. A series of winter storms kept us in port for almost two weeks. When I returned to my trap line, all but twenty of my traps were gone; swept ashore in wads of giant kelp and destroyed in the surf zone. No one was spared; everyone had lost most of their gear to the storm; we all got serious about protecting our remaining gear.

The morning news carried a story about a surfer shot at La Jolla Cove. He was entering the water at one in the morning when he was shot in the leg with a high-powered rifle. His companion rushed him to the hospital several blocks away and he survived. I knew the backstory; One of the guys fishing the La Jolla Cove sector had been getting robbed from the beach. He was going broke and decided to put an end to it. The shooter was never identified.

Things took an ugly turn just before the season closed; a guy in the Bird Rock sector was caught poaching traps belonging to his fellow lobstermen. This touched off a buoy-cutting skirmish. A quick sure way to destroy another lobster fisherman was cut off his marker buoys. A few slices with a sharp knife and the gear below was lost forever. I too was being robbed on a regular basis. Trader Vic had given me his sawed-off shotgun before he left for the Air Force. The stock had been cut down to a pistol grip making it resemble a pirate's flintlock. I took five shells, dumped out the shot, and loaded them with rock salt. The loaded shotgun rode in a holster on the port gunwale of my skiff for the rest of the season.

We also had an equally serious problem as the end of the season neared. Bait for our traps, abundant earlier in the season, was in critical short supply. I occasionally found drowned Cormorants and Surf Scooters in my traps which I removed and tossed overboard. Now any bird that happened into a trap was chopped up and put into the bait cage. Any and all household scraps ended up in the bait cage. I was forced to make my own bait in the end. The Quivira Basin bait barge attracted schools of Queenfish that were easy to catch and made good lobster bait. When the Mission Bay bite slacked off, I was forced to motor around the Point to make bait at Brock's San Diego Bay barge.

I was returning from Brock's with a nice load of Queenfish in the late evening with just three weeks left in the season. I brought Whiskey along for company. He was always eager to go to sea but got left home for his own safety. The dog got in the way on the small skiff when I was throwing around heavy pieces of gear. The bait gathering trips were different with no traps aboard.

I made the mistake of trying to cut the corner at the tip of Point Loma and wound up weaving my way through the dense kelp bed off the lighthouse. I was a hundred yards from clear water when the engine died. I found the propeller shear pin had been severed. Also, the cooling water intakes were plugged by kelp causing the engine to overheat. I could fabricate a shear pin I thought, but would the engine start? After a half-hour of pulling on the starter rope, I had my answer; the motor was dead, and I was in a pickle. To make matters worse, I had slammed my hand into the motor cowling trying to start the engine; I now had a bleeding laceration across the knuckles of my right hand. I tore a strip of cloth from my shirttail and wrapped the hand as best I could.

I sat down to catch my breath and noticed the skiff had drifted far from where the motor stopped. There was a running tide coming out of San Diego Bay carrying me toward the ship channel and out to sea. I deployed a small shallow-water Danforth anchor with fifty feet of rode to no avail. It was dark now and I was getting chilly. I pulled Whiskey up onto my lap and hugged him tight. The distant lights of San Diego twinkled in the cold night air. Looking to sea I saw nothing; no lights of an approaching ship, just blackness.

I was getting hungry. I had fresh Queenfish and rock salt and a thermos full of coffee left over from the morning. Squinting in the dark, I filleted two Queenfish on the center seat, then pried open one of my five shotgun shells and coated the raw fillets with rock salt. Even though I had good reason to be, I wasn't worried yet; I enjoyed my makeshift meal and washed it down with cold coffee. Next, I chopped up a Queenfish for Whiskey and gave him a drink of water from our canteen. He jumped back on my lap; this time I let him inside my shirt. His head popped out of my flannel shirt next to mine; we road up and over the dark swells in silence keeping each other warm.

I was staring at the distant twinkling lights on the Silver Strand when I heard a noise behind me; it was buoy number one, the Whistler Buoy marking the entrance to the bay and I was drifting directly toward it. If I could just snag it and tie up, I could stop my drift to sea. I rummaged around in the bottom of the boat and came up with a single sixty-foot trap line and a single brick ballast bloc. We were quickly approaching the buoy, passing just a few yards to one side. I had one chance as we slid by; I swung the brick around and released. The bloc splashed down three feet short. I watched in silence as the Whistler fell away astern. My hand was bleeding and throbbing now from the failed attempt. I tore a fresh strip of cloth from my shirttail and wrapped it tight around the wound tight to stanch the bleeding.

I had never felt so alone in my life. I thought of the laughter and happy times at Ma Kellogg's Clubhouse with my friends, now all in uniform and scattered around the globe. Trader Vic was a crewman on an airborne early warning and control aircraft flying missions over Vietnam and the Gulf of Tonkin. Gale was in Germany. Kenji was in training in Colorado, and Mouse was in the Air Force stationed in New Mexico. Carl was an infantryman on the ground in Vietnam, as was his friend Kimo. Swabby Don was in Germany, and Tinman was in Vietnam with the Navy.

I was starting to despair, thinking about my family. They needed me, they depended on me. I couldn't die out here. They were probably getting worried by now and had called the Coast Guard to come find me; it was my only hope. I caught glimpses of the twinkling lights of Imperial Beach and Tijuana from atop each swell before sliding into the pitch-black trough. I was shivering now and struggling to keep my head about me. Whiskey joined me inside my flannel shirt again and I hugged him tight. He wasn't the least bit concerned; his Master was holding him close; everything was right with the world.

The current was taking us further south. I reckoned we were directly offshore from the Tijuana Bullring when I got to my feet to pee. I glanced back to sea; there was a speck of light in the blackness; a star low on the horizon perhaps. I sat down, opened my shirt and Whiskey crawled back in. My thoughts turned to the unsolved killing of the Swindle couple at the Silver Spray seawall. The mysterious Bart Walters had become a major drug trafficker. He made frequent trips across the desert to the border town of Nuevo Algodones near Yuma, returning with bricks of Mexican pot to sell in San Diego. On a recent return trip Walters pulled out to pass a line of cars on US Route 80 just east of El Centro. He was hit head-on by a fully loaded Peterbilt semi tractor-trailer and died instantly. It was rumored that the semi's front bumper sheared off the top of the car taking Bart's head off at the shoulders. Regarding the Swindles; what he knew, or didn't know, would now remain a mystery.

I stood up to stretch and look out to sea. The point of light I had seen earlier had grown; it wasn't a low star it was an approaching vessel. I uncased the binoculars and watched the point of light intently until I could make out the running lights; the green was on my left, and the red on the right: It was coming directly toward us! The veteran lobstermen had told me at the outset to invest in a flare gun; advice I ignored. Now I was kicking myself in the ass for coming to sea so unprepared. Nothing had ever gone wrong; until now.

As the ship approached, I could see more detail. It was not a Naval vessel, but it was quite large. Through the binoculars I could make out a submersible tied to the aft deck. I had seen this vessel many times before at the Scripps complex near Kellogg Street; it was a new research ship, the *David Starr Jordan*. I crossed my fingers and said a prayer as she approached; I glassed the deck looking for crew. I spotted several seamen working on the stern. I had to somehow get their attention.

I went to the gunwale and unholstered the sawed-off shotgun. Several minutes later the ship was upon us, sliding by several hundred yards away. I loaded the first shell and fired into the night sky, then quickly followed with a second and then a third. I had two rounds left. I said a prayer and fired the fourth round. My prayer was answered; I could see a commotion on the fantail of the *David Starr Jordon*; I could hear the engines reversing. Suddenly racing spotlights were sweeping the sea surface all around the *Flora Wynn*. I had one shell left; the one I had emptied of rock salt. I fired the last round and was immediately bathed in light.

R/V David Starr Jordan

I could see a small boat being lowered into the water. A
short time later the launch came alongside, and the
coxswain hailed; "Are you okay?" I answered; "I'm fine
now that you're here; just cold and hungry!" The launch
took the *Flora Wynn* in tow and delivered me and the dog
to the mothership. I put Whiskey under my arm and
scrambled up the boarding ladder where the Captain and
several crew members were waiting. I was immediately
wrapped in a blanket and taken below. The ship's medic
cleaned and bandaged the laceration on my hand. The
cook brought a ham sandwich and hot coffee for me and
a bone for Whiskey. I was overwhelmed by their
kindness and concern; they were as happy to have found
me as I was to be rescued. We pulled into the Scripps
dock awhile later. The launch towing my dead skiff
landed at the Harbor Police dock on the other side of the

channel and left her there.

I was offered a ride to the hospital to be checked out. I declined but accepted a ride to Quivira Basin where my wagon was parked. I drove back to the Shelter Island Harbor Police dock where my boat was impounded. After answering a few questions, I was given permission to leave the skiff at the impound dock until I could arrange to trailer it home. I climbed back into the wagon just before sunrise and headed home. I found the family sound asleep; I had not been missed. There had been a function at Ma's place the night before I was planning to attend. The family assumed that's where I went after work and all was well. No one was looking for me. The crew of *David Starr Jordon* likely saved my life. It was a sobering conclusion that marked the end of my days as a commercial lobsterman.

I left Whiskey at home and drove to the old Point Loma lighthouse to watch the sunrise. I came here often to reflect; the vast Pacific Ocean stretched out in all directions. It was a cold, clear morning. The Mexican coast was visible from the Tijuana bull ring all the way to the power plant by Rosarita. The familiar outlines of Los Coronados Islands stood out crisp and clear on the horizon.

I was done with fishing. There were only three weeks left in the season, my boat was dead in the water, and I had been rattled by my experience; never again would I go to sea without the most basic safety equipment. I had twenty pieces of gear still positioned off Sunset Cliffs. I would offer them to Mr. Detweiler, a neighbor and veteran lobsterman who helped me get started. I left the lighthouse and drove to Pete's for the comfort of his company, and a hot Danish fresh from the oven. Just being alive that morning was exhilarating.

13 HARD TIMES

Peace Love & Dope

I sold my skiff, as is, to a neighbor who was looking for a project boat. With that, I was done fishing and no longer employed. Because of the draft it was nearly impossible to find work. Employers were reluctant to spend time and money training a new employee only to lose them to the draft a few months later. I would soon lose my deferment; I had already made the trip to the Los Angeles Armed Forces Entrance Examination Station for my physical exam. For the family, money was tighter than ever.

To make matters worse, Whiskey was not well. He was as sweet and attentive as ever, but increasingly stiff, slow to move, and in pain. No one knew for sure how old the dog was. He could have been close to the end of his life when I adopted him. Perhaps it was a blessing that the end came suddenly one Saturday afternoon under the wheels of a Helms Bakery truck. The driver never saw him hop off the curb, reverse direction, and run beneath the rear tires of his truck. The driver, well known to the family, was distraught and in tears. I sat on the curb and held Whiskey until the light in his eyes went out.

Whiskey had endeared himself to all who had gotten to know him. He had become best buddies with my neighbor's shepherd mix, Cricket; she followed Whiskey everywhere he went. Cricket was at my side on the curb when Whiskey passed and had been visibly distraught ever since. Most of my friends were in uniform and gone. Those few who were still in OB came to the house that evening. We fashioned a casket out of a cardboard box. I wrapped the body in Whiskey's favorite bed blanket and placed it in the box. My twin brothers Jerry and Garry were eight, and my sister Donna, ten. Using their crayons, they drew hearts and flowers on the cardboard coffin. My friends added peace symbols and brief messages. We opened the woody's tailgate and slid Whiskey in for his last ride. The funeral procession left Pescadero bound for Ladera Street and the Cal Western wilderness.

We parked at the top of the hill and set out for Ab. It was a cloudy full moon night; our entourage of nine mourners and Cricket the dog cast long shadows on the dirt trail as we walked in silence. It was eerily quiet: The only sounds came from our footfalls and the clanging of the picks and shovels we were carrying for the burial.

The spot I had chosen for the burial was just above the chute leading down to the beach at Ab. It was hard sandstone and difficult digging. We took turns with a pickaxe busting out a grave deep enough to be safe from scavengers. We lowered Whiskey into his final resting place around midnight. My little sister Donna said a prayer, then we took turns sharing Whiskey stories. The full moon, on the horizon now, created a shining path on the surface of the sea. At the conclusion of a round of sweet tear-jerking recollections, we rounded up our tools and headed for home. Whiskey's buddy Cricket refused to leave the grave and had to be picked up and carried out.

There seemed to be no end to the bad news. A week after losing Whiskey I received a letter from Carl who was now in Vietnam. The staff and children at Rancho Esperanza had been summarily evicted to make way for development of the planned high-end resort, golf course and marina. The resident orphans were hurriedly parceled out to sister facilities in Ensenada and Tijuana. Carl's parents had temporarily relocated to their trailer in San Miguel to assist with the transition. A handful of senior staff led by Senora Ulloa held peaceful protests in the face of the bulldozers, refusing to leave the main sanctuary. They were arrested and jailed for their disobedience. Local sympathizers and legal-minded members of the Collins' congregation were working to free them.

By the late '60s drugs had come to Ocean Beach in a big way. OB had the dubious distinction of being commonly referred to as Haight-Ashbury South. Stoners from less tolerant parts of the country began showing up in droves. The distinctive smell of burning marijuana and incense hung heavy in the air everywhere in the North Beach neighborhood, the so-called "Combat Zone". North Beach must-have furnishings included one or more black lights, brick and board shelving, throw pillows for the floor, a mattress to sleep on, and the most expensive sound system one could afford.

It was the era of turntables and the LP vinyl record. The sounds of Janis Joplin, Jimi Hendrix, Jefferson Airplane and the Grateful Dead, were heard at all hours of the day coming from North Beach houses, apartments, and courtyards. On lower Newport a new kind of business opened; the Paisley Pelican was a place where stoned locals and drifters could gather for, among other things, strobe light shows. Sitting back against the wall watching people dance in the strobe beam was a transporting experience. I was at my third such event when the strobe touched off a brief episode that scared the hell out of me; I didn't know what had happened, only that I was conscious but not in my body for a moment. I avoided flashing lights from then on. It would be years before I learned the cause was photosensitive epilepsy, aggravated by cannabis.

The widespread acceptance of marijuana in the underground opened the door to experimentation with other drugs. This did not end well for many folks. Barbiturate and opiate overdoses, some fatal, began occurring on a regular basis. For some stoners, amphetamines became the drug of choice. Speed freaks were easy to pick out of the crowd; disheveled and malnourished, covered with scabs from incessant scratching and picking, nervously grinding their teeth. Most potheads tried the LSD experience, but it was a different trip altogether, and not suitable for everyone.

Hippie Days on Newport

It was during this time that I first saw people sleeping on the beach and in the local parks. The average street person was young and had recently arrived from somewhere else. Their primary means of support was panhandling along the beach and at the foot of Newport Avenue. They were annoying but mostly harmless; more than a few were juvenile runaways.

Soon after losing my deferment I received orders to report to AFEES Los Angeles for my second physical; induction was sure to follow. I began preparations to leave. I sold the woody to one of the Hundhausen brothers, sold my Fender Mustang guitar and amp through the Union Tribune classifieds, and left my boards and dive gear in the keeping of my siblings. It was two weeks before my report date when I was leveled by the Hong Kong flu. I had never been so sick in my life. I spent close to a week in a feverish delirium wracked with debilitating body aches. My request for a postponement of my second physical was granted. It took two full weeks for the flu to run its course. I was left weak and shaky in its aftermath, my body thoroughly depleted from the fight.

A nagging pain in my abdomen sent me in to see Dr. Greaves. Test results offered no clue as to what the problem was. The following morning the pain was worse, and I was running a high fever. That evening I was admitted to Doctor's Hospital and prepped for emergency surgery; my appendix had burst during the night. I woke

up in the recovery room in the wee hours of the morning;
I was packed in ice and a masked nurse was holding my
hand. I spent the next two weeks in the hospital fighting
for my life. Coming on the heels of a virulent flu, my
ruptured appendix came close to doing me in. I would
spend another two months convalescing at home before
returning to a normal existence.

Out of this episode of frightening misery came something
good. I spent a lot of time on the seawall at the foot of
Newport during my convalescence enjoying the ocean
and chatting with locals and tourists. One afternoon a tall
skinny guy about my age plopped down next to me and
introduced himself as Pete. Pete was ecstatic; he had just
come from Mission Gorge where he had scored
admission to an Army Reserve unit headquartered
adjacent to Admiral Baker Field in San Diego. There
were still a handful of openings according to Pete, but
they were going fast. I returned home and did some
quick phone work, followed by a next day visit to Van
Deman Hall Army Reserve Center; I was in. I would
eventually be sent to Fort Bragg, North Carolina, then
tidewater Virginia, then home to Camp Pendleton to do
reserve time.

The rough patch of hard times ended on a happy note:
My neighbor came to me during my convalescence with
the exciting news that Whiskey's girlfriend Cricket was
pregnant. When the big day arrived, both families
huddled around Cricket's bed in the neighbor's garage to

watch the birth. Our neighbor kindly gave us pick of the litter. The first pup out was a female, identical in every respect to her father except for her Dad's birth defect. We named our new little girl "Whiskie", a feminized version of Dad's name. She would become part of the family and live to the ripe old age of fifteen.

Whiskey's Little Girl

14 THE WORLD CLOSES IN

South Ocean Beach Before the Pier

In the early '60s the City of San Diego embarked on a project to build a fishing pier that would extend seaward from the foot of Niagara Avenue. Public reaction to the project was overwhelmingly positive, both in and out of OB. On July 2nd, 1966 California Governor Pat Brown led an entourage of VIP's in a ribbon cutting ceremony that opened the pier to the public. A celebration at the foot of Newport Avenue was attended by a crowd estimated to be ten thousand strong. Almost immediately, the pier became one of the most photographed landmarks in San Diego County; it put OB on the map. The pier accelerated what would ultimately be profound changes in the character of Ocean Beach and its residents; the days of our Mayberry by the sea were coming to an end.

Barely two months after the pier ribbon cutting ceremony, the third ISF World Surfing Championships were held in Ocean Beach over a one-week period; September 29th through October 4th. The best surfers in the world representing seven nations descended on OB putting our little village on the world stage. In the surfing world the 1966 contest was a watershed event.

Up until that time the primary contest maneuver by which contestants were judged was nose riding. The master of the nose was a California transplant from Oahu, David Nuuhiwa; he was heavily favored to win the men's division of the OB contest. The inventive Australians had been experimenting with shorter more maneuverable boards. Australian standout Nat Young came to the contest with a transitional board he named Magic Sam. His radical slashing style won him an unbeatable lead in points with two days left in the contest. Favorite Nuuhiwa was eliminated, despite an unheard-of toes-over nose ride lasting 10.1 seconds.

The pier was immediately a huge success for locals and outsiders alike. It was the longest concrete pier in the world upon its completion, reaching offshore to the inner edge of the kelp forest. A restaurant and bait & tackle shop near the end provided anglers with all their needs. For the first time San Diego anglers with disabilities or bound to wheelchairs by age could enjoy independent deep sea fishing; and it was free. The only thing I had against the pier was its location smack dab in the middle of my favorite summer wave. You could still catch the lefts off the rocks and "shoot the pier" but the break was forever changed.

Skip Wright & Pier in Progress

There was another public project in the works that would have an equal, if not greater impact on OB; the extension of the Interstate 8 freeway from Old Town to Sunset Cliffs Boulevard. Before the Ocean Beach Freeway, it was necessary to navigate through city streets in the congested Midway-Rosecrans area and enter the community on West Point Loma Boulevard. We were no longer isolated by being "out of the way"; the I-8 freeway brought the world directly to our doorstep.

Rumors began to circulate that the City of San Diego was planning another major project in Ocean Beach to be carried out by the Army Corps of Engineers. The south jetty of the Flood Control Channel was going to be extended for the purpose of protecting north OB from flooding. On the surface it appeared to be a good thing. During periods of heavy winter rains, flood waters could make it around the stubbed jetty and threaten homes on lower Muir, Voltaire, and West Point Loma Boulevard. Extending the jetty five hundred feet or so would channel the floodwaters into the sea and mitigate the threat to North Beach residents.

When specifics of the project began to emerge the surfing community was horrified. The jetty was not planned to end at the water's edge, but continue over fifteen hundred feet into the sea, then hook south toward the pier creating a huge lagoon. Now the swells that had forever fired the peaks of Ocean Beach would die in a brief surge against the new breakwater. Ocean Beach was ahead of its time as an ecologically aware community. Opposition to the jetty extension grew rapidly and included residents of all age groups. By the summer there would be fighting in the streets as a ragtag army of OB townsfolk took on City Hall and the Army Corps of Engineers in a David and Goliath matchup.

To some, the project appeared eerily familiar to the methodology used to create Dana Point Harbor four years earlier. The headland at Dana Point had been a premier big wave spot for years. "Killer Dana" held form during the heaviest swells. To the chagrin of local surfers, construction began in 1966 on the breakwater that would turn Dana Cove into a still water lagoon. Then came a marina that would eventually be home to over two thousand boats, waterfront dinner houses, and high-end lodging. The possibility that such a fate would befall Ocean Beach was unthinkable; an existential threat.

Another worrisome aspect of the project was the dredging of the sand plug at the San Diego River mouth after the jetty extension was complete. The bowl-shaped peak at the jetty was arguably the best wave in Ocean Beach. It would be destroyed by dredging operations. The dredging would be the first step in realizing a desire by certain interests to make the San Diego River navigable all the way to the SR 163 bridge.

The Fashion Valley Mall was under construction. Al Speise was an apprentice illustrator from Alpine. He moved in next door to me and we struck up a friendship. Al worked for a contractor to the Hahn Group creating marketing literature. Al had seen a pamphlet with an artist's concept drawing of mall patrons shopping by boat. The drawing depicted a mooring basin at the SR 163 bridge with a dozen guest docks for shoppers. Al also claimed to have seen a rendering of a three hundred slip marina on the site of the Stardust Country Club golf driving range. The low bridges at the Sunset Cliffs and Midway Drive crossings effectively blocked all but the smallest sailboats. Shallow draft power boats on the other hand could easily navigate the new five-and-a-half-mile waterway.

I stepped into the fray for the first time at the OB Recreation Center. A public question and answer session was underway, hosted by City officials to inform and win support for the project. It was a warm summer evening. Inside the Rec Center it was standing room only. Outside a hundred or more late comers milled about on the steps and sidewalk straining to hear what was going on inside. The Project Engineer from the Army Corps was the keynote speaker. He was hammered repeatedly with questions for which he had no answers. The City officials present cowered to a corner of the stage and let the ACE spokesman take all incoming arrows. I remember feeling a bit bad for the guy; he had been thrown to the lions and the lions were hungry.

Down at the beach a lay down yard had been established for the granite boulders and heavy equipment needed to put them in place. The jetty-making process started with creation of a deep hole into which the foundation boulders would be placed. As soon as the work crew left for the day, we began filling in the hole they had just dug. Working all night, an army of OB rebels filled in the hole by hand, leaving the workers to start from scratch again. Still, we were losing ground. Then someone had the brilliant idea of digging a channel from the new hole to the sea. The incoming sea water caused the sides of the hole to collapse and fill the hole naturally. Just the same, we continued to lose ground and it became clear a new tactic was needed. That was when things began to get ugly.

Over the course of the next few weeks the heavy equipment was occupied, vandalized, and set afire. Rock throwing was now a routine occurrence. Granite stones in the lay down yard provided an abundance of ammunition. The police were now fully involved, declaring unlawful assemblies, setting up skirmish lines and making arrests. The clashes with police culminated in an all-out riot in July. I was put off by the escalating violence caused largely by a handful of bad actors among the protesters. On the night of the grand finale we watched things unfold from the roof of Billy Mills' duplex on Long Branch Avenue. When the melee was over, close to thirty protesters had been arrested and scores of cop cars had busted out windshields and smashed headlights. The efforts in the trenches did not stop the jetty, but it bought valuable time for the OB groups pursuing a legal remedy to wend their way through the system.

Ringside Seat

In the end the Army Corps of Engineers conducted a reevaluation which concluded that stopping the jetty at the water's edge was sufficient to mitigate flooding in lower OB; no extension was needed. OB residents of all stripes had stood up to the political machine at City Hall, and the Army Corps of Engineers, and prevailed. The following year a City ordinance was passed prohibiting any future extension of the jetty beyond its final terminus at the water's edge.

To me, the jetty war marked the end of the Ocean Beach I grew up in, and the beginning of something new. Sprawling new suburbs in Mira Mesa, North Claremont, and Tierra Santa were drawing young families inland, to affordable tract homes in child-friendly neighborhoods.

Many established families stayed on in Ocean Beach, but it was rapidly becoming a population of college students and newcomers that occupied OB proper. Newport Avenue businesses that once provided everything a family needed began to falter as patronage of the new commercial districts of Midway-Rosecrans and Mission Valley grew. Newport Avenue would eventually morph into a drinking and eating destination for San Diego residents and tourists. Sandwiched between the new eateries and places to drink were numerous antique stores housed in storefronts that formerly provided some useful product or service. This was neither good nor bad, it just was; not the end, but another step in the evolution of a more inclusive Ocean Beach.

Welcome Home

Of course, more people meant more problems; more crime, a dramatic increase in homeless folks living on the beach and in park shrubbery, and traffic congestion every sunset evening with droves of visitors flocking to the Sunset Cliffs turnouts or to the pier to try and catch a Green Flash. Despite all this, there remained an unwavering opposition to the gentrification that had destroyed the character of many Southern California beach towns. That spirit remains to this day.

I often speculated over the years that there must be some sort of magnetic anomaly that manifests under the soil and in the air of Ocean Beach; like a Bermuda Triangle thing. It calls out to free spirits everywhere who, upon finding it, know they are home at last.

EPILOGUE

Lloyd Kenji Kozuma 1946-2019

Our dear friend Kenji Kozuma passed away in September 2019 after a lifelong career in dentistry. His brother Gene Kozuma passed one month later. Sister Gerry is a retired Master Cruise Planner still living in San Diego.

Carl Collins became a medical doctor specializing in infectious diseases and is still practicing in various parts of the world with Doctors Without Borders. Carl never married. Kimo Kahale returned to Oahu after serving in Vietnam. Kimo went missing on a huge day at Sunset Beach in 1976 and was never seen again; it was his thirtieth birthday.

Trader Vic is retired and living in Wildomar, California. Mouse Marions is still in Ocean Beach; out of the Combat Zone and up on the hill. Tinman Tinsley lives in Lakeside, California. All are now well into their '70s; grandparents and great-grandparents.

Sadly, the beautiful deep lagoon at the end of the San Diego River is gone; the lagoon and river channel filled in with sediment over the years and is now a vast mudflat. On the upside, the new configuration created an ideal shallow-water hunting ground for Ospreys; a magnificent bird that is now a common sight.

The single 45 recorded by the Inmates in the '60s resurfaced in the United Kingdom in 2010 as a northern soul collector's item. Discs in good condition continue to fetch several hundred dollars each.

Mister Liticker's Liquor Store continues doing business at the same location on Voltaire Street under the same name. Likewise, Chris' Liquor has endured the test of time and continues to thrive under the management of Chris' son Greg. On Newport Avenue the venerable Pacific Shores Bar doesn't look much different than it did when it first opened its doors in 1941.

Whiskie was a treasured member of the Phillips family for fifteen years. She was put down in 1983 when the ravages of old age finally overtook her.